I0530123

SISI SURGANT

BURN BEAUTIFUL

From Burn Scars to Bold Fashion: What One Immigrant Woman's Story Can Teach You About Power and Possibility

LITTLE BLACK BOOK

PUBLISHING

St Louis, MO

PRAISE FOR

BURN BEAUTIFUL

Sisi is an incredible woman with an influential story. Multifaceted, driven and without a doubt, inspiring. Her book, "Burn Beautiful" is a double entenderé, one that shares her story as a burn survivor and the beauty of overcoming through perseverance, but also a reminder that as women, we all have to undergo the fire to become who we were truly meant to be!

— **Chelsea Haynes** | On Air Host at KTVI FOX 2

I loved reading the inspirational story of Sisi, what she has overcome and her self discovery along the way. It's a story of determination, tenacity and her decision to face life's twists and turns with a positive outlook and a smile. I can't recommend her book enough.

— **Mary Clarke** | Co-Founder Mother Model Management

Sisi Surgant became a fast friend the moment I slid into her DMs with a bold idea—asking if she'd MC my St. Louis book tour event. I had no clue then just how deeply our lives would intertwine, but I did know from the start: this woman is special. Sisi is the kind of woman who makes you feel like anything is possible—and then shows you exactly how it's done.

Reading "Burn Beautiful" felt like sitting front row to her soul. It's raw. It's powerful. And it's one of the most human things I've ever read.

From the opening scene of her standing on stage, medal around her neck, disbelief coursing through her body, you're instantly pulled into a journey that's about so much more than bodybuilding or business. This is a story about rising, not in spite of your scars, but with them. It's about what happens when a woman refuses to shrink in the face of pain, fear, or self-doubt, and instead dares to be seen.

Sisi doesn't just tell her story; she hands you the ability to tell your own. Every chapter ends with a "Reflect Ritual," an invitation to pause, speak truth into the mirror, and remember who you are. As a reader, it's not just something that inspires you. It's something that truly allows you to rise.

What Sisi has built on stage, in business, and through her brand, MISAJO SPORTS, is nothing short of a movement. But what makes her so magnetic is that she leads with heart. I've seen her show up for women again and again. As a mother, wife, stylist, and survivor, she is proof that you can carry both softness and strength, and still stand tall.

If you've ever felt invisible...If you've ever been told you're too much or not enough...If you're standing on the edge of a dream but afraid to leap, this book is for you.

Sisi, thank you for showing us what it means to rise and for reminding us that success isn't about perfection. It's about powerfully returning to yourself, again and again.

This book isn't just a good read, it's a revolution.

Let's rise.

— **Amanda Riffee** | Bestselling Author, *Unleashing You* | CEO | Certified Expansion Coach

"Burn Beautiful" is a heartfelt journey through the life experiences of Sisi, told with humor, optimism, and unwavering authenticity. Through her stories, she offers powerful lessons on rising above obstacles, rejecting the limitations others try to place on us, and courageously following the inner light that guides us to our purpose. Every page is infused with her passion, and her voice shines through with clarity and strength. Sisi is truly an inspiration to all.

— **Angel Magasano** | Bestselling Author, *Success Matters* | Founder, Little Black Book Women in Business

As a fellow burn survivor, reading Burn Beautiful hit deep. I know what it feels like to battle those silent insecurities and still show up in the world with courage. Sisi's words reminded me of the power in our scars and the beauty in our truth. Her story feels like mine in many ways, and I know I'm not the only one who'll see themselves in these pages. This book is real, raw, and full of life."

— **Kanisha Anthony** | Burn Survivor and Author of *Scarless: A Women's Journey to Finding Her Strength and Identity* | Model | Digital Creator

Published by LBB Publishing. An imprint of Little Black Book: Women in Business

Cover, interior design, and editing by Shelly Snow Pordea

Cover photo by Kevin de Miranda

Paperback ISBN 978-1-962417-32-7

Ebook ISBN 978-1-962417-31-0

Hardcover ISBN 978-1-962417-33-4

LITTLE BLACK BOOK
PUBLISHING

CONTENTS

"Respond to every call that excites your spirit."

— Rumi

INTRODUCTION

THE SPOTLIGHT

And then they call my name.

My leg is shaking. My arms are shaking. My smile is so wide, I'm convinced I'll need medical attention later. Honestly, it feels like my face could power the whole auditorium. What am I doing here? Seriously. *What am I doing here?* I'm standing on this huge stage, lights blazing down so brightly, I swear they're trying to blind me, with a sea of people staring at me. A whole row of judges is sitting there, analyzing every inch of my body.

Me. A mom of two.

Me. A stranger in this country who is sometimes still trying to pronounce words the right way or even find the right translation.

Me. Someone who has spent her life in the background, watching other people win.

Me. A double immigrant.

Me. A burn survivor, whose scars tell a story most people never even ask about.

And here I am, on this stage, wearing a bikini that leaves almost nothing to the imagination. Not even my cellulite gets a free pass tonight.

And then I hear it: "Third place."

At first, it didn't compute. Third place? Me? Did they really say my name? Either I haven't heard right or—as usual in life—they don't know how to pronounce my name. My brain is doing cartwheels while my body just stands there, trying to look cool, like I'm not two seconds away from ugly crying.

Someone hangs a medal around my neck.

A medal. I've never held one of these in my life—not unless you count the times I held other people's awards. And now here it is, shining around my neck. My heart feels like it's about to burst, and suddenly, I'm overwhelmed by this tidal wave of emotions: joy, disbelief, pride, gratitude, you name it. I want to scream, "I did it!" so loud that the ceiling collapses.

But I also want to laugh hysterically, because—let's be honest—who would've ever guessed this would be my moment? Me. Winning a bodybuilding competition medal! Wtf?

And yet, standing here with a medal around my neck, I know this is only part of the story. Because now? Now I'm the founder of a successful fashion brand that empowers women with internal and external scars. I'm a cover girl. A public speaker. A bodybuilder. A stylist who has styled over a thousand women and celebrities, helping them feel powerful in their own skin. The woman behind Styling with Sisi, a monthly TV styling show. I've been featured in magazines, podcasts, and TV segments—and the brand is expanding beyond the U.S.

Women from all walks of life—mothers, survivors, creatives, CEOs—gather around this work like it's a movement. And maybe it is. Women of all ages, sizes, backgrounds, and stories come together not just to dress up, but to rise up. It's not about perfection. It's about rising. And somehow, the girl who once felt invisible is now the woman helping others be seen.

For a split second, I think about all the things that brought me here, the sleepless nights, the fear, the scars, the determination, the moments I almost gave up. How did this even happen? How did I get from there to here?

This is the proudest "me" moment of my life.

But to understand why, we have to rewind.

We have to go way back to the beginning, to the moments that built this one.

The funny, messy, painful, and beautiful ones.

Before we dive into the stories that shaped me, I want you to know this book isn't just something to read. It's something to experience. Because you're not just holding my story. You're holding space for yours.

After every chapter, you'll find a simple but powerful moment of reflection.

I call it the Reflect Ritual—a practice to help you pause, reconnect with yourself, and rise in real time. It's not about perfection. It's not about journaling for hours (I mean, you totally can if you want to). It's about taking a few quiet minutes to look yourself in the eye and say: *I'm still here. I still matter. I'm still rising.*

So, before we rewind to the beginning, let me show you how we're going to walk through this book together.

HOW TO USE YOUR REFLECT RITUAL

This isn't homework. This is soul-work.

This book is about rising—from pain, from pressure, from stories that tried to shrink you. But reading isn't enough. You need to feel it. See it. Say it.

That's why, at the end of each chapter, you'll find a simple, powerful practice called the Reflect Ritual—a moment to pause, reconnect with yourself, and rise in real time.

You don't need a journal. You don't even need to write anything if you don't want to.

All you need is:

- A mirror

- Your phone

- A quiet space

- A few minutes of honesty

Here's how it works:

The Ritual (Do this each time)

1. Find your mirror. Stand or sit in front of it. Look yourself in the eyes.

2. Open your phone. Use your voice memo app or video camera. Hit record.

3. Say the prompts out loud. Each chapter will give you a few powerful sentence starters. You finish them. In your voice. Your way.

4. Save your recording in a folder called "I Rise."

Yes, really. Create a folder. This becomes your personal library of rising moments. Go back and listen anytime you forget how powerful you are.

Optional: Write it down.

Need help? I got you. All chapters will include a QR code. Scan it, and I'll guide you through the Reflect Ritual myself—like your own private hype woman in your ear.

Each ritual ends with one optional sentence you can write right in the book. If you're a pen-to-paper kind of girl, do it. If not, skip it. You're still doing it right. This is your moment to speak the truth. To speak it out loud. To speak it into your mirror. Because when you speak power into your reflection, you don't just see yourself differently. You become her.

Now turn the page. The first chapter and your first Reflect Ritual are waiting. Let's rise.

Our roots run deep, even when we grow in foreign soil.

— Sisi Surgant

Chapter One

THE BEGINNING

I was born and raised in Germany. In beautiful Munich, a city that will always have my heart. But before I could call Munich home, it was the place where my parents, both immigrants, met and started building their lives.

My mom: a fiery Moroccan woman with a personality that could fill any room, and my dad: a cool, laid-back Tunisian who balanced her energy perfectly, crossed paths there in 1973. They were both in their early twenties, far from home, and full of big dreams. Together, they created a life rich in love, laughter, and resilience—a foundation that shaped everything I am today.

Life in Munich was... complicated. Being part of an immigrant family meant living in two worlds at once. At home, it was all Moroccan and Tunisian traditions, full of flavor, rhythm, and ritual.

Every Sunday, my mom made couscous. And not just any couscous—*the* couscous. The kind that made my friends beg to come over. She was a magician in the kitchen, turning spices and love into something unforgettable. Arabic TV blared in the background while she sang, danced, and turned our home into a one-woman musical—every week.

My mom? She was the mother of moms, strong, unstoppable, and always open for a good joke, even while juggling a thousand things at once. She worked multiple jobs, made three meals a day, and still somehow had time to ask if I'd done my homework. (Spoiler alert: I usually hadn't.) Honestly, I don't think she ever slept. I mean, maybe she did, but how would we know? She just kept going; always with a smile, always loud, and never complaining. She wasn't just a mom; she was a life coach, therapist, chef, and drill sergeant all in one.

But here's the thing about my mom—she didn't do pity parties. If I came home crying because some kid bullied me, she wouldn't sit there going, "Oh, poor baby." Okay, maybe sometimes, but most of the time, she'd say, "Why are you letting them talk to you like that? Stand up for yourself! Talk back! Don't let anyone treat you like trash!" Honestly, sometimes she made me feel like being bullied was my fault, but in her own way, she was teaching me to be fierce. She's the reason I know how to stand tall today.

And then came the hamam bath. But don't picture a relaxing spa day or bubble bath with candles, no, this was serious business. My mom scrubbed us down with a Moroccan kees, the rough glove that made sure no layer of dead skin survived. It didn't hurt exactly, but it definitely wasn't a spa day. It was "you'll be clean if it's the last thing I do" kind of love.

And oh—the hair. Washing this thick, North African hair of ours was a whole operation. Detangling, deep washing, brushing, styling—it was a process. She took it very seriously. After the bath, she'd wrap old tights around our ponytails to make the hair smooth, flowy, and "less wild." Western kids have no idea—they'd hop out of their bubbly baths, let their hair air-dry, and somehow look runway-ready the next day. Meanwhile, we were going through Olympic-level grooming just to make it to Monday. Hoy yoy!

Every bath came with a story. Every story came with a song. And somehow, even when I rolled my eyes, it all felt like home. Saturdays were for cartoons and coziness, wrapped in the scent of spices and laughter. That was our world.

And then outside—was Germany. Efficient. Modern. Quiet. A little cold at times, but still beautiful. Germans take their seasons seriously, their schedules even more so. And one thing I'll say: I've never seen a country so clean. Trash bins everywhere. And somehow, everyone actually uses them.

Germany was neat, predictable, and structured. But life? Life doesn't always follow the rules. And just when things felt simple on the outside, my own story was carrying something far more complicated on the inside.

It was like Germany raised me, educated me, shaped me... and still kept me at arm's length. Back then, especially in the 80s and 90s, diversity wasn't celebrated—it was tolerated. You learned to overcompensate. To shrink a little. To prove, without anyone asking, that you deserved to be there.

I was a kid, going to school, trying to make friends, living life—and still always felt like I had to apologize for something I couldn't put my finger on. Like my name, my hair, my parents' accent, or the food in my lunchbox was a problem I had to solve. And the strangest part? I didn't even know about another home. Sure, we visited Morocco and Tunisia every year, but Germany? That was my home.

My dad, on the other hand, was my rock and my comfort. He is a teddy bear of a man with the warmest, most giving heart I've ever known. He never sugarcoated anything; if he had something to say, you'd hear it, whether you wanted to or not. But he had this incredible ability to balance that bluntness with an endless capacity for love.

He couldn't see any of us cry, especially me. If I was upset, he was the first to hug me, wipe my tears, and say, "Nobody is going to make my daughter cry." In the moments he held me, the world felt safe again. And he could never say no to me. All I had to do was ask nicely, and whatever I wanted was mine. I might've taken advantage of that once or twice (or more), but hey, I was the youngest, and I wasn't about to waste that privilege!

Both my parents made me feel that no matter what happened, I'd always have someone in my corner. And that family is everything! My siblings? Well, they were kind of amazing, which made growing up both inspiring and wildly frustrating.

My sister was like a human Swiss Army knife—smart, beautiful, and so independent that it made the rest of us look bad. She was the family's lawyer, accountant, therapist, and probably the CEO, if we're being honest. My parents relied on her for everything, and so did I. She was my German mom before I even realized I needed one. My parents, being immigrants, couldn't really help me with school or with a lot of the things that had to be managed in Germany, but my sister always tried to step in. When we were younger, we didn't always get along—because *siblings*—but as I grew up, she became my safe haven.

She was always there, helping me navigate the weirdness of growing up in Germany and trying to fit in, which in our case, meant learning how to laugh off the awkward stuff while still quietly wondering if we actually belonged.

And in the middle of all that confusion, of feeling invisible and too visible at the same time, my sister was always there. Four years older, wiser, and always ready to translate the unspoken rules of belonging. She couldn't shield me from it all, but she stood beside me, loud and proud, like my personal bodyguard against the feeling of being too different. And sometimes, just knowing she was there made the weight of not fitting in feel a little lighter.

My brother was the eldest, and basically the mayor of Munich—or at least, that's how it felt. Everyone knew him. He was so talented, a well-known dancer and rapper, and he was extremely respected (in school, classmates even carried his books). He was cool in a way that made me want to be him and roll my eyes at him all at the same time. He loved being the oldest, which meant he also loved being in charge. He was so overprotective of us that my sister and I used to hate him for that, but deep down, we knew he'd always have our backs.

Now, picture me in the middle of all this greatness. My brother, the local celebrity. My sister, the family genius/beauty queen. And then there was me: the awkward youngest kid with burn scars and hair that refused to behave. My siblings were so cool and so talented that I'd stare at them like, "Are we sure we have the same parents?"

But I had one thing they couldn't take away from me: stage presence. Oh, I could perform. Singing, dancing, acting, you name it, I was there. Was I as good as them? Debatable. But in my little world, I was Left Eye from TLC or Pepa from Salt-N-Pepa.

It wasn't always easy, but my parents made sure we never felt like we were missing out.

There was something that made me feel smaller than anything else ever could. It was my scars, proof of a moment I was too young to remember but would carry with me forever. You see, when I was just one year old, life decided to throw me a curveball. I became a burn survivor before I even knew how to say my own name. It's a story that shaped everything about me, but back then, it just felt like a cruel twist of fate.

And if I'm going to tell you how I got from that baby to the person standing on a stage in a bikini, we have to rewind a little more to that moment—the one that changed everything before I even understood what "everything" was.

THE LESSON & REFLECT RITUAL

The Lesson:

Your beginning doesn't define your limits.

You can carry scars and still carry power.

You can feel like an outsider and still belong to yourself, to your people, to your purpose.

Let's get practical.

It's time to rise.

REFLECT RITUAL – CHAPTER 1: The Beginning

"Where I Come From, and What I Carry"

Your Tools:

- A quiet space

- A mirror

- Your phone (open voice memo or camera)

- 3 minutes of courage

Your Reflect Ritual (Say these out loud):

1. "The people who raised me taught me..." (Maybe it was resilience. Maybe it was survival. Maybe it was how to fight, cook, laugh, or never give up.)

2. "What I carry with me today is..." (Maybe it's love. Maybe it's pressure. Maybe it's both. Say what's real for you.)

3. "The part of me that felt 'too much' or 'not enough' as a kid was..."(Be honest. Name it. Say it like you're talking

to your younger self.)

4. "But today, I see that version of me and I say..." (This is your MirrorTalk moment. Say something healing. Speak with power and softness at the same time.)

5. "I rise because..." (End with this. Let it come from your gut. Let it land.)

Optional:

Write this in your book: "This chapter reminded me that I am..."

Need support?

Scan the QR code to hear me guide you through this Reflect Ritual. You're not alone in this. I'll walk you through it, breath by breath.

Maktoub

Arabic: "It is written"

CHAPTER TWO

THE RAINY DAY THAT CHANGED EVERYTHING

May 18th, 1985. It was a rainy Saturday, the kind of day that makes you want to stay home. The skies were dark, the rain relentless, and the occasional bursts of hail pelted against the car windows as my parents drove. I was just a one-year-old, strapped into the car with my siblings—my ten-year-old brother and my five-year-old sister.

My parents weren't even sure they should go anywhere. My mom actually got very angry about it, and they debated turning around a few times, but they felt a sense of obligation. A family friend was in the hospital, and they wanted to visit him. It didn't feel right to back out, so they kept going despite the bad weather.

What I'm about to share isn't something I remember; it's a story told to me over the years by my mom, dad, and siblings. I was too young to recall any of it, but their memories of that day are vivid. It's a story that shaped not just my life but all of theirs too.

After arriving at the hospital and spending some time with the friend, my parents decided to stay longer. The friend's wife was alone at home with their kids and felt lonely, and the family friend convinced my parents to keep her company. My dad had to run a quick errand, so he left my mom, my siblings, and me at the friend's house for a while.

I was thirteen months old, sitting next to my mother, on a little chair in my own little bubble of baby thoughts. My sister, five at the time, was playing nearby with our mom's friend's daughter. The two of them were giggling and twirling around, caught up in their own world, until their game got a little too wild. At some point, they picked up a metal bar to play with, and my mom, always quick to react, jumped up to take it away before anyone got hurt.

And in that split moment—while her eyes were on the girls—everything changed.

The family friend stepped out of the kitchen carrying a tray of freshly brewed Moroccan tea. The kind that's super hot and sweetened with thick sugar. She spotted me sitting on the chair and, for reasons I'll never truly understand, thought I was about to fall. That's what she says, at least. So she rushed toward me to grab me, and in the chaos, the tray tipped.

I don't remember any of this—I was too little—but I've imagined it a thousand times. The boiling tea spilled all over me. The scalding sugar clung to my skin. It burned my chin, my chest, my belly, the inside of my legs, and other parts of my tiny body. I don't remember the pain, but the scars tell the story.

The only reason my face was spared is because of my big brother—my ten-year-old hero—who acted fast. They say he knocked the rest of the tray away before it could reach me. I don't remember that either, but I know in my bones that he protected me. He always did. And even though I don't say it enough, I'm so deeply grateful. For that moment. For every moment. For the way he's always shown up for me and still does.

We've always had a bond that words can't fully explain. He's not just my brother—he's one of the first people who ever fought for me.

We don't remember the moments that define us. Not when we're that little. But they shape us anyway.

According to my mom, the room exploded into chaos.

She remembers screaming. Crying. Not the kind of crying where you're still composed, but the kind that pours out from the soul. The kind that comes from watching your baby suffer in a way no mother ever should. The friend who spilled the tea was in complete shock, apologizing over and over again, frozen in place. My siblings—just kids themselves—were terrified. Still. Silent. Eyes wide, unable to process what they were seeing.

And me?

I was crying, my mom said. Wailing in a way she had never heard before. A cry that wasn't just from pain—it was confusion, fear, betrayal by the world around me. My skin blistering, my baby body burning. My tiny world—my soft, safe baby bubble—shattered in seconds. I didn't understand what was happening, but my body did. My nerves were screaming. My soul was stunned. I was in agony, and I didn't even have the words yet to ask for help.

The ambulance came quickly. But the burns were severe—third degree. There was no time to wait. I was rushed to the hospital, and after a quick assessment, they realized I needed care beyond what they could provide. Arrangements were made to transfer me to another facility.

My parents have told me about that moment many times. About how surreal it was to see their baby—barely over a year old—being taken away like that. My life was hanging in the balance, and there was nothing they could do except pray and trust strangers to save me.

But there's one detail my mom always comes back to.

She says when they laid me down for transport, one of the medical staff—maybe a nurse, maybe a doctor, no one remembers now—sat beside me. And I didn't cry. I didn't make a sound. I just reached for him. My little baby hand grabbed the fabric of his shirt, held on tight, and didn't let go. I stared at him in complete silence, wide-eyed, stunned. Like my body had used up all its noise. Like all I could do was hold on to something—someone—and try to survive.

That image haunts my mom to this day. Her baby girl, burned and broken, clutching a stranger in total silence.

That was the moment she knew things were serious. That this wasn't just an accident—it was a trauma that would live with all of us forever.

I spent the next six weeks in the ICU.

Six weeks of wires, tubes, beeping monitors, and sterile white walls. Six weeks where my little body had to relearn everything it had just barely begun to know. I had to learn how to eat again, how to move again, even how to walk.

I couldn't take anything by mouth at first, so they fed me through tubes. When I was finally able to start tasting again, it was with tiny Q-tips dipped in juice. I would suck on them like a baby bird, one drop at a time—just enough to feel something sweet in the middle of all that pain.

My mom never left my side. Not for one second.

She stayed in that hospital room day and night, holding space for me while juggling everything else. She had to be my rock while still being a mother to my siblings. She was fighting fear with every breath, doing everything she could to make sure I felt safe. And even now, all these years later, when she tells me those stories, she still cries. Her voice trembles, her eyes fill with tears. Because even though I don't remember it... she does. Every second.

She let my brother and sister play in the hospital playground because, in the middle of all this heartbreak, they were still kids. She watched them through the window—her body inside the ICU, her eyes outside on them. Always checking, always hoping they were safe. I can only imagine what that must have felt like—being torn in three different directions, but still showing up fully for all of us. Carrying the weight of my pain, their innocence, and her own guilt for not being able to protect us all at once.

And my dad... he tried to hold everything together. He had to keep working, keep showing up, keep the family afloat—financially, emotionally, spiritually. He bounced between the hospital, home, and work, carrying his trauma in silence, while trying to be there for his wife, his burned baby girl, and his two other children, who didn't fully understand what was happening. He had to be the strong one. But I know it broke him, too.

There was a moment—my mom always brings it up—when one of the doctors looked at her and said, "You know... your daughter's baby fat may have saved her life."

Before the accident, she used to get told all the time that I was too chubby. That I was overweight. That she needed to stop feeding me so much. But ironically, that extra softness—the rolls, the roundness, the cheeks everyone loved to pinch—that might have been what kept the burns from reaching my organs. That softness became armor.

And my mom? She's proud of it. Still. She says, "I fed you so well, baby, I saved your life."

The scars, though, were unavoidable. They stayed. But so did I.

The burns didn't just change me.

They changed all of us.

That day rewrote my entire family's story.

My parents carried—and still carry—a mountain of guilt. Even now, all these years later, they still replay the what-ifs in their minds like a never-ending loop. What if I had been faster? What if I hadn't looked away? What if I could go back? What if we hadn't gone to visit that day?

The weight of those questions broke some of their relationships, too. We no longer speak to the family friend who caused the accident. Not because we didn't try—but because the pain was too deep, the wounds too raw. Some things just couldn't be repaired. There was too much grief, too much blame, and too much sadness sitting between everyone like an invisible wall.

My siblings were just kids, but their childhoods were stolen in an instant.

Suddenly, everything became about me. About poor Sisi. About getting me better. About hospital visits, burn creams, special care routines, follow-up appointments, and making sure I wasn't in pain. They were little—but they had to grow up fast. And even though no one ever said it out loud, I know their hearts carried confusion, jealousy, sadness... maybe even guilt of their own. Everything shifted. And they were left figuring it out in the shadows of my recovery.

For a long time, I didn't feel guilty. I just saw myself as the victim. The little girl who got hurt. The one who was scarred. I didn't know any better.

But as I got older, the guilt crept in. Quiet at first, then louder. Even though I know it wasn't my fault, I started to feel ashamed of all the attention. I wondered if I was worth all the sacrifices my family made. The time, the energy, the emotional toll. My siblings had to grow up faster than they should have. My parents' lives were consumed by my care. And I sometimes asked myself... was I worth it?

And still, when I think of that little baby me, just 13 months old, sitting on a plastic chair one second and wrapped in bandages the next... I can't help but wonder what she went through. What she felt in that moment. What she still carries in her body.

Because I know I carry it.

And something in me changed as I got older. Especially now, being a mother myself.

I started to see my parents differently. When they used to cry while telling the story, I would roll my eyes and think, Oh come on, I'm fine. Why are you overreacting?

But now? As a mom myself.

Now I get it.

Now I feel it in my bones.

Now, when I think of my mom watching her baby suffer, juggling two other kids, she could only watch through a hospital window, trying to smile while dying inside—I want to cry for her. I want to hug that version of her and say, You did so much. You did enough.

I started to see my siblings differently, too. I used to be so caught in my own pain, I couldn't see theirs. But now I do. They were just kids, trying to make sense of why everything changed. Why their baby sister suddenly needed so much. Why their parents were tired and tense, and always busy with me.

And believe it or not... I even started to empathize with the woman who caused it all.

The family friend who made the mistake.

She didn't wake up that morning planning to pour boiling tea on a baby.

But it happened—and it changed her life too.

How do you live with something like that?

It took me years to realize that my scars weren't just mine. Everyone around me carried pieces of them, too.

Empathy became the shift that changed everything for me. It softened the sharp edges of my pain and reminded me that I wasn't the only one carrying it. My parents, my siblings, even the woman who accidentally burned me—they all carried their own version of the trauma. Just because their scars weren't visible didn't mean they weren't wounded.

When you begin to see the story from more than just your perspective, something powerful happens—you stop feeling like you're carrying it all alone. The weight is still there, but somehow, it becomes more bearable when it's shared. That's the quiet magic of empathy. And if there's one thing I believe the world desperately needs more of, it's that—the willingness to feel for each other, with each other, beyond just ourselves.

May 18th, 1985, a rainy Saturday that changed everything. It is the reason I'm a burn survivor, the reason I have these scars. But it's also the reason I've learned to appreciate resilience, love, and the strength of family. It became my superpower. It was a very dark day in my life and my family's life, but it taught me some of the most important lessons I carry with me today.

I no longer look at May 18th as a sad day. I actually celebrate my resilience and my strength that day, kind of like a second birthday.

THE LESSON & REFLECT RITUAL

The Lesson

Your pain may be personal, but healing takes a village.

Sometimes the people around you are carrying pieces of your story, too—even if their wounds don't show.

When we begin to see others through the lens of empathy, our story doesn't shrink—it expands.

And that's how we stop carrying it alone.

Let's get practical.

It's time to reflect and rise.

REFLECT RITUAL – CHAPTER 2: The Rainy Day That Changed Everything

"The Scars We See... and the Ones We Don't"

Your Tools:

- A quiet space

- A mirror

- Your phone (open voice memo or camera)

- 3 minutes of courage

Your Reflect Ritual (Say these out loud):

1."A moment that shaped me, even if I didn't fully understand it then, was..."

(It could be a trauma. A shift. A memory you carry. Let it come up gently.)

2."What I carried from that moment was..."

(Fear? Guilt? Strength? Speak it out loud. No judgment. Just truth.)

3."Someone else who was also impacted by that experience was..."

(This is the empathy piece. A parent. A sibling. A teacher. Name them.)

4."When I think of them now, I realize..."

(Say what you see now that you didn't see then.)

5."I rise because..."

(End with power. Speak it from your heart. Let it land in your bones.)

Optional:

Write this in your book :

"This chapter reminded me that healing is..."

Need support?

Scan the QR code to hear me guide you through this Reflect Ritual.

I'm with you. You don't have to carry your story alone.

I am not what happened to me, I am what I choose to become.

— Carl Jung

CHAPTER THREE

THE BATTLE OF THE OUTSIDER

When I was six, I thought the world was about to change for the better. I was so ready to start first grade and leave all the chaos of kindergarten behind. I was tired of the loneliness, the teasing, and feeling like I was invisible. Kindergarten had been a special kind of nightmare. I didn't speak the language. I didn't understand the culture. I was like a fish out of water, gasping for air while everyone else seemed to be swimming just fine.

And then there was Patrick, that little jerk. Every day, he'd call me "chocolate" because of my skin color, making me feel like I was too different, too foreign to fit in. He also teased me about my hair and called me "Sun" because it stuck up like I had a solar panel on my head. He made kindergarten feel like hell.

I also didn't have a single friend. No one wanted to play with the brown girl who barely spoke German, who stood out in every way, and who didn't understand the games or the jokes or the rules. I get it now—how do you play with someone who doesn't even speak your language? But back then, it just felt like I wanted to be invisible. Or worse, like I was wrong.

I remember sitting on the sidelines while everyone else paired up. I was the outsider. Always left out. And when I found my courage and tried to speak up, tried to explain to the teachers, in my broken baby German or with desperate hand motions, that Patrick was calling me names, they just shrugged and said, "Then call him vanilla." No discipline. No compassion. Just a joke. As if a five-year-old could defend herself from daily bullying with some witty comeback. All I probably wanted was protection.

It's funny, I don't remember a single other kid's name from that class. Not one. But I remember Patrick. It's wild how the people who hurt you the most can carve their names into your memory like they paid rent to stay there.

So, when first grade came around, I thought, This is it. Finally, a new beginning! I was so excited. I was going to be in the same school as my siblings, and best of all, my best friend, who also happened to be my neighbor, was going to be in my class. We were going to be like a dynamic duo! Everything was going to be different.

As I already mentioned, I could barely speak German. I knew maybe five words. Yep, five. That's like trying to communicate using the equivalent of "hi," "bye," "apple," and some random phrases from cartoons. Not exactly a conversation starter. But, for some strange, innocent, and naive reason, I felt very positive about that. I thought it would be enough. Sweet baby me.

So there I was, already one foot in the "outcast" category without knowing it. And of course, I was struggling just as before to fit in, and the bullying from Patrick still echoed in my mind. It felt like I couldn't catch a break. First grade was supposed to be a fresh start, but I felt like I was stuck in the same old loop of embarrassment, confusion, and loneliness.

I wasn't just an outsider at school. I was the outsider outsider. So unpopular that my sister, who was four years older than I was, actually had to force kids to play with me. Like, force them. God bless her heart, she tried so hard. She'd go up to kids in my class, probably begging them to be nice to me. And my brother? He was in ninth grade, already the coolest and the most popular kid in school. He would straight-up push other kids around to protect me. As if the cool factor of being his younger sister was going to work some magic. Spoiler alert: it didn't. No matter how hard they tried, no matter how much they had my back, I was still that girl no one really wanted to be around. I was just the "not cool" kid.

I never had any of the school kids come to my birthdays. The only ones who showed up were my family and my one friend, my neighbor. How sad. I think you get how unpopular I was. School was just not fun for me.

And then... as if it couldn't get any worse... the slap.

I'll never forget that moment. The teacher told us to be quiet and focus on our worksheet. I raised my hand because I had a question. And then, out of nowhere, there it was—the slap that felt like it defined my entire existence at that school. My teacher, who was supposed to be a mentor, a guide, a protector—she slapped me across the face. Hard. I mean, what kind of person does that to a six-year-old? Especially a kid like me, who was so shy I barely said a word.

I remember it vividly. I sat there, stunned, my cheek on fire, my eyes welling up with tears. All I could do was hide my face and put it down on the table. I didn't look up for the rest of the day. I felt embarrassed, humiliated, scared, and ashamed. And the worst part? I probably thought it was my fault, that I deserved it. I felt like I was disappearing right there, swallowed up by the humiliation. Not only did I not belong, but it felt like I was the target for all of it: my teacher slapping me, the kids avoiding me, mocking me, or pretending I didn't exist.

And the worst part?

I never told my parents.

Not about the slap. Not about how small and ashamed I felt.

Looking back, I think I didn't tell them because I truly believed it was my fault. Like, somehow, I had done something wrong—like I was the problem. I wasn't just the unliked kid... I was the worst student in the class. The one who never had the right answers. The one who always got everything wrong.

Now I know why.

I didn't speak the language. I didn't understand the language. And no one could help me at home. I wanted to do the work—I wanted to be a good student—but I didn't even know what I was supposed to do. I didn't even know how to ask for help. And no one showed me. No one knew how to help.

I just remember sitting there, holding in tears, feeling like a failure. Feeling like a disappointment. Like I was already too far behind to ever catch up. I couldn't bear the thought of telling my parents. I couldn't stand the idea of letting them down again. I just kept it all inside.

And I remember thinking, my face must be swollen. I was sure I had a black eye. I didn't—but that's how it felt. Like the shame had made its way under my skin. Like it was bruising me from the inside out.

And what haunts me the most is this:

Who slaps a six-year-old child?

Who raises their hand against someone so small, so lost, so eager to be good, but just in need of help?

Anyway, the days went by. Year after year. And yep, I was still the uncool kid. Still the outsider. Still the girl nobody really wanted to be around. I had gotten used to that feeling, that quiet ache of not being liked, not being picked, not feeling smart or special. I didn't expect much. I just wanted to get through school, day in, day out, without being noticed.

Until that day came.

I was in fourth grade.

And it flipped something in me. Hard.

There was this girl, a fifth grader. Everyone knew her. She was kind of a legend at our school. Rumors said she had a black belt in karate. I still don't know if that was true, but it didn't matter. She walked around like she owned the school, fierce, confident, and absolutely untouchable. Even my sister liked her.

But me? I didn't like her.

Because, honestly? She wasn't nice. Especially not to me.

She was kind of a bully, not in-your-face aggressive, but sneaky, smug, and sharp. She knew how to make people feel small without saying much. She never had a kind word for me. Just little digs, rolled eyes, and that kind of look that made you feel like you didn't belong.

And if I'm being totally honest with myself... deep down, I was probably jealous, too. Jealous that people liked her. Or feared her. Or gave her the attention I never got.

So one day, during lunch break, I made a dumb comment to one of my classmates. Something like, "Ugh, I'd love to beat her up."

It wasn't serious. I wasn't planning anything. I was just venting. Blowing off steam in the only way my fourth-grade brain knew how.

But guess what my brilliant classmate did?

Yep. He ran straight to her and told her everything.

And just like that, I went from being invisible to being the girl who "talked trash" about the most feared (and probably most watched) girl in school. It spread like wildfire. She loved it. This was her moment, her invitation to humiliate me, and she took it gladly. She made it a whole event. She literally told everyone, "Fight at recess!" Like it was a show.

She was thrilled.

She already didn't like me. She'd made that clear a few times before in her little bully ways. And now, she finally had her golden opportunity to put me in my place. I was terrified. She had that energy, you know the kind. That fire that told everyone not to mess with her. Me? I was just... scared. Soft. A mess inside.

So there we were.

The crowd circled around us like it was a WWE match.

And I remember thinking, What the hell have I done?

I stood there, heart pounding, completely frozen. I didn't know how to fight. I had no idea what to do. But something in me: panic? Anger? Exhaustion from always being the one who got walked on?, snapped.

And in that moment, I decided: I'm not backing down.

We lunged at each other. And it was a mess. No form, no technique. Just two kids, fighting like maniacs. I was hoping not to get knocked out. She was probably hoping to make an example of me.

But then... something surprising happened.

I won.

I actually won.

Don't ask me how. Maybe it was dumb luck. Maybe I had just hit my breaking point. Maybe all the rage of being invisible finally gave me a wild kind of strength. But I walked away from that chaotic little storm of a fight... victorious.

And for the first time in my life, I felt powerful.

People started talking to me. Seeing me. I wasn't the forgettable, weird, scarred girl anymore. I had made my mark, messy and wild as it was. I had stepped out of the shadows, even if it was for something I never expected.

But let me pause here and say this loud and clear:

I do not support fighting. I don't believe violence solves anything. I'm not proud of what happened that day. I don't think that's the right way to earn respect. And I would never, ever tell anyone to do what I did.

I was a kid. A scared one. And I did something dumb that spiraled into something bigger than I could handle. I'm sharing this because I want to be real with you. Vulnerable. Honest. This is not a proud story. But it's part of my story.

And if I'm being even more honest?

Now, as an adult, I actually feel sad for both of us.

Me, the invisible girl who thought a fight was the only way to be seen.

And her, the girl who felt so powerful putting others down. Who knows what she had to go through to become the kind of kid who bullied others just to feel important?

We were just two hurting kids. That's all.

But in that moment, I didn't see it. I just needed to fight for something. For myself. For that little voice inside me screaming, Enough!

And even though I'd never wish to repeat that day, it did something to me. It flipped a switch. From that moment on, things started to shift. I wasn't the outcast anymore. I wasn't invisible. My lonely birthday parties? A thing of the past. I had earned my way into the crowd through the most unexpected, messy, chaotic path possible.

And it wasn't pretty.

But it was mine.

That moment showed me that even the smallest spark of courage, born out of fear, pain, and desperation, can start something powerful. And though I didn't fight again after that (and never plan to), that day gave me a piece of myself I'd never had before:

A little taste of my own strength.

THE LESSON & REFLECT RITUAL

The Lesson

The moment you decide you're worth standing up for—even if it's messy—is the moment you stop disappearing.

Your confidence doesn't have to be perfect. It just has to be real.

Sometimes, as kids, we act out of pain instead of power. But even those moments can teach us how to rise with compassion.

Let's get practical.

It's time to reflect and rise.

REFLECT RITUAL – CHAPTER 3: The Battle of the Outsider

"The Day I Stopped Shrinking"

Your Tools:

- A quiet space

- A mirror

- Your phone (open voice memo or camera)

- 3 minutes of courage

Your Reflect Ritual (Say these out loud):

1. "A time I felt like I had no voice was..."

(Was it at school? In a relationship? At home? Let it come out. No shame here.)

2. "What I believed about myself in that moment was..."

(That I didn't matter? That I wasn't enough? That I had to prove my worth to be seen?)

3. "But what I needed to hear back then was..."

(Speak gently to your younger self. Offer her the love and protection she didn't have.)

4. "The moment I stood up for myself looked like..."

(It may not have been perfect. Maybe it was full of fear. That's okay. It was yours.)

5. "I rise today because..."

(This is your power statement. Say it clearly. Say it like you mean it.)

Optional:

Write (your version of) this in your book:

"This chapter reminded me that strength can look like setting boundaries, breaking silence, or choosing to see others with empathy—even when they didn't see me."

Need support?

Scan the QR code to hear me guide you through this Reflect Ritual.

Let's rise together. You're not alone in this.

A girl should be two things: who and what she wants.

— Coco Chanel

Chapter Four

THE JUDGE WHO NEVER WAS

In Germany, when you're in elementary school, you don't just have different teachers for each subject like in some other countries. Nope. You get one teacher for two full years. Two. Full. Years. Meaning, if you're lucky, you get a wonderful, inspiring, warm-hearted teacher who makes you feel like you can do anything.

And if you're me... You get the exact opposite.

For the second time in my short school career, I had a teacher who was cold, unfriendly, and anything but encouraging. She wasn't the type who saw potential in kids and nurtured their confidence. She was the kind who probably enjoyed reminding kids that life was hard, and dreams? Well, those were reserved for other children.

By this time, I thought I already knew a few things about myself:

1. I wasn't smart.

2. I wasn't beautiful.

3. I wasn't popular.

4. I had scars on a large area of my body from the burn accident.

That was my identity. That was my reality. And the world, especially the world of school, did nothing to make me think otherwise.

And then came the moment.

It was one of those classroom exercises where the teacher asked everyone what they wanted to be when they grew up. A classic. One by one, the kids eagerly shared their dreams. Some wanted to be doctors. Others wanted to be teachers, engineers, or even astronauts. Big, bright-eyed dreams, filling the classroom with excitement.

And then it was my turn.

Now, let me tell you something. Speaking in class was not my thing. It took everything in me to even open my mouth. But this was about my dream. And my dream? I wanted to be a judge. Not a lawyer. A judge. The person who makes the final decisions. The one with authority, wisdom, and power to bring justice.

So, I gathered all my courage and said it: "I want to be a judge."

And that's when it happened.

The teacher misheard me. She thought I said I wanted to be a poet (which, in German, sounds similar to the word judge).

"A poet?" she asked, raising her eyebrows.

I shook my head, my face burning. "No, a judge."

She looked at me. And then, right there, in front of the entire class, she laughed.

Not a haha, how funny, I misunderstood you kind of laugh. No. It was the kind of laugh that tells you you're ridiculous. That your dream is absurd.

Then she looked me dead in the eyes and said: "You better choose a different job because you will never achieve this."

Boom. Just like that. No sugarcoating, no gentle letdown. Just pure, blunt rejection.

She continued, as if explaining something completely logical: "You are not made for this. With your circumstances, you are never going to become a judge. This dream is not for you."

Now, let's take a second here.

I was nine years old. Nine. And there I was, already struggling with feeling different, feeling less than, feeling unseen. And this woman, this teacher, whose job was literally to teach and uplift children, just looked me in the eyes and told me my dream was not for me.

Not for kids like me.

Maybe for the German kids. Maybe for the ones who came from richer families. Maybe for the ones who were already excelling in school. But for me? Absolutely not.

I sat there, swallowing the lump in my throat, trying not to let the tears rise to my eyes. I nodded like I understood. Like I accepted it. Like I agreed.

And the saddest part? I did.

Because this wasn't the first time someone told me I wasn't good enough. And it wouldn't be the last.

Spoiler alert: I didn't exactly finish school on a high note. That moment with my teacher didn't just sting—it settled into my bones. It became one more reason to believe the story I was already telling myself. I'll share more about how things unraveled later, but let's just say: the system wasn't built for girls like me—immigrants, scarred, and constantly underestimated.

Years later, I decided I'd had enough of carrying that unfinished story. So I went back to school. As a grown woman, I returned to school in Germany to re-earn every single degree, one by one. And in Germany, there's no shortcut. You don't just take one big test like the GED and get a diploma. No, you start where you left off, all over, fully. You go back to the classrooms, the exams, the pressure, and fight your way through the entire system to be allowed into university. It was one of the hardest things I've ever done—but also one of the most empowering.

Until the day it wasn't.

It was supposed to be different this time. I was no longer a child. I was grown, wiser, and I had lived enough life to know that I was capable. That I was intelligent. That I had a right to take up space.

And yet.... There I was again, an adult, back in school, determined to earn my degree. I had worked so hard to get here. Surrounded by younger classmates, I sat in that classroom day after day, raising my hand, answering questions, contributing with confidence. History was my thing; I knew the material. I was serious, focused, and committed. But no matter how hard I tried, no matter how often I showed up and spoke up, I kept getting a C.

And every single time, Veronica—the sweet girl who sat next to me, who had openly told me more than once that she didn't know much about history—walked away with an A. Over and over. Until one day, I couldn't take it anymore. I stayed after class and asked the teacher, respectfully but directly: "Why do I always get a C? I'm not trying to sound arrogant, but I know this subject. I participate. I study. I care."

She looked at me with the kind of calm certainty that cuts deeper than anger. The same certainty I recognized from a different lifetime—my fourth-grade teacher, who once believed she had the power to define my worth. And then she said it.

"Sisi, you can't compare yourself to Veronica. She's German. You are not."

Just like that. As if it were the most logical explanation in the world.

I felt it all over again—the sting of being othered. The humiliation of being unseen, unheard, misjudged. The silent, suffocating rage of knowing that no matter how hard I tried, how much I proved myself, someone would always find a way to remind me: You don't belong.

I wish I could tell you I stood tall and gave her a piece of my mind. But I froze. All I managed to say was, "How dare you?" My classmate, who had stayed behind with me, was just as stunned. "I can't believe she said that to you," he whispered.

But I didn't report her. Because deep down, I knew nothing would happen. Back then, teachers still held all the power. And I had already learned one of the hardest truths of my life: Some people don't need a reason to believe you are less. For them, simply being you is reason enough.

Looking back, I realize that these moments weren't just about a teacher crushing a kid's dream or playing favorites. It was about something much bigger.

It was about self-belief. Or, in my case, the lack of it.

For so many years, I had already felt like I wasn't smart enough. I wasn't good enough. And when adults, especially people in authority, kept reinforcing that idea, it just became my truth.

That's what childhood is, really. It's a collection of experiences that slowly shape the way we see ourselves. And in my case, school was one long reminder that I wasn't meant for great things. That my dreams were too big for someone like me.

These moments weren't isolated. They repeated. Different faces, different settings, but the same message: This is not for you.

But let me tell you something: They don't get to decide.

Not them. Not your teachers. Not your family. Not society.

Only you get to decide what the eff... You are made of!

And if I could go back in time and sit next to little nine-year-old Sisi, I would whisper in her ear:

"Fuck her, fuck all those teachers. You become whoever you want to become, and you will."

THE LESSON & REFLECT RITUAL

The Lesson

Just because someone has power doesn't mean they're right.

When someone tells you your dream isn't for you, that says more about them than it does about you.

Your voice matters. Your presence belongs. Your dream is still valid—even if you were the only one who ever saw it.

Let's get practical.

It's time to reflect and rise.

REFLECT RITUAL – CHAPTER 4 The Judge Who Never Was

"When They Said I Couldn't—But I Did Anyway"

Your Tools:

• A quiet space

• A mirror

• Your phone (open voice memo or camera)

• 3 minutes of courage

Your Reflect Ritual (Say these out loud):

1. "A time someone in authority made me feel small was..."

(Maybe it was a teacher, boss, parent, or coach. Name the moment. Speak the truth.)

2. "What I believed about myself after that was..."

(Maybe you thought you weren't smart, worthy, capable, beautiful, enough. Say it—even if it still stings.)

3. "But what I now know is..."

(Flip the script. Speak the truth that little you needed to hear. Let your mirror catch the power in your eyes.)

4. "That dream they laughed at? It still matters because..."

(This is your moment to reclaim what was stolen. Say it like it's already yours.)

5. "I rise because..."

(Say it like a declaration. Let it ring.)

Optional:

Write this in your book:

"This chapter reminded me that my dreams are…"

Need support?

Scan the QR code to hear me guide you through this Reflect Ritual.

Let's speak power into the mirror, together.

Joy is a form of rebellion when the world tries to shrink you.

— Sisi Surgant

Chapter Five

THE MAKING OF A SUPERSTAR... ISH

WORLD TRAVELER'S EDITION

Okay, enough with the sad stories, let's talk about the star that almost was.

Because let me tell you, little Sisi was destined for fame.

I wasn't just your average kid. Oh no. I was a singer, a rapper, a dancer, an actress, a model—all rolled into one. I was ready to take over the world, but the world just didn't know where to find me.

If reality TV talent shows had existed in my world back then, I would've been all over them. The only problem?

They never told you where to go.

I mean, come on! How was I supposed to send in my audition tape for the Mini Playback Show if they didn't tell me where to send it? A major flaw in the system, if you ask me. Or maybe I was just too young to figure it out. Deep down, I always wondered—what if someone had helped me? What if someone had noticed that this little girl, hidden behind burn scars and insecurity, had the fire and the flair to light up a stage?

But still... that didn't stop me.

Salt-N-Pepa *who?*

Let's talk about my rap career. Because yes, I had one.

I was convinced—convinced—that my best friend (aka my neighbor, Mona) and I were better than Salt-N-Pepa. You couldn't tell us anything. Our masterpiece? Push It. We had the moves, we had the energy, and most importantly, we had the attitude.

Did we ever perform it anywhere? Absolutely not.

Did we practice like we had a world tour coming up? Absolutely yes.

We were in my bedroom, hyping each other up, working on our flow, making sure our moves were on point. If someone had handed us a microphone and a stage, we would've shut it down. No doubt.

But rap wasn't my only talent. Oh no, I was also a dancer.

Let me set the scene. It was first grade. There was a school dance competition. My big brother was a dancer, my sister was basically a professional choreographer, and they both made sure I was ready for this moment (especially my sister).

Mona and I showed up looking iconic—matching denim overalls, because obviously, we understood fashion before the world did.

→ Me: blue sweater, blue bandana.

→ Mona: red sweater, red bandana.

We danced to Bobby Brown, and let me tell you—we delivered.

There were more kids in the competition, but eventually, it came down to the two finalists: us and one older kid in sixth or seventh grade, thinking he had it in the bag.

He didn't.

Because we showed up and shut it down.

And we won.

That moment? One of the happiest moments in my rough school years. For once, I wasn't the kid with scars or the kid who didn't belong. I was the one who stood out—in the best way.

And even though nobody else saw it yet, I felt it.

In that little bubble—my bedroom, the dance stage, my imagination—I was safe. I was alive. I was whole.

And that's the power of joy.

When the world tries to crush you, and you still choose to sing, to dance, to imagine—that is your soul fighting back. And mine? Oh, mine fought hard.

Because even though I was already being bullied, already learning to shrink, already hiding parts of myself just to get through the day—these moments? These were the ones where I didn't have to shrink. Where I remembered who I was underneath it all.

That joy? That was my inner child in full bloom, reaching for the sun anyway.

If you think my talents stopped at singing, dancing, and rapping, think again.

Because I was also an actress and a model. My sister and I spent hours filming movies on our old family camera. And when I say movies, I mean movies. We had storylines. We had costumes. We had drama. My sister was the director, the scriptwriter, the visionary.

And I? I was the star.

We even edited them. If it were today, we would be Instagram super-creators. We had full-on modeling sessions, too. My sister would record me walking like Naomi Campbell, posing like I was in Vogue, swinging my hips like I was born for the runway. And honestly?

I was born for it.

Too bad social media wasn't around back then, because we would've gone viral.

As I look back, I realize—those weren't just fun childhood games. That was my purpose starting to speak. That was my light refusing to go out.

Those were the moments that planted the seed for the woman I am today.

The one who believes the sky isn't the limit—it's just the view.

The one who helps other women believe they can do anything.

The one who rushes to open doors, to show the way, because she remembers how badly she needed someone to do that for her.

No grown-up in my world back then knew how to help a little girl become a superstar.

They loved me, yes. But they didn't know the path.

No one showed me how to enter that world. How to get seen. How to follow the spark.

And so, I built my own spotlight.

And now?

Now I use it to light the path for others.

Because when a child believes in something that strongly—even if it never made it on stage—that kind of belief never dies.

It just grows up, gets a little louder, and one day...

It writes a book.

THE LESSON & REFLECT RITUAL

The Lesson

Your inner child didn't need permission to shine.

She didn't ask for a spotlight—she created one.

Joy is power.

Creativity is resistance.

And those childhood dreams?

They were never silly. They were seeds.

Even when no one cheered, even when no one opened doors, you danced anyway.

You sang anyway.

You believed anyway.

And that fire? It didn't burn out.

It became the very spark you use to light the way for others now.

Sometimes the most powerful thing you can do is protect your joy.

Even when the world doesn't see you, doesn't validate you, or doesn't "get" you—you've always been magic.

Joy is not a luxury. It's your legacy. And it's a form of resistance, of healing, and of returning to who you've always been.

REFLECT RITUAL – CHAPTER 5: The Making of a Superstar

"Joy Is My Birthright"

Your Tools:

• A quiet space

• A mirror

• Your phone (open voice memo or camera)

• 3 minutes of courage

Your Reflect Ritual (Say these out loud):

1. "A time I felt fully alive and free as a child was..."

(Think of your little self doing something joyful—singing, imagining, swimming, dancing, drawing, dreaming.)

2. "What I believed about myself in that moment was..."

(Did you think you were talented? Magical? Unstoppable? Say it now.)

3. "The world didn't always see me, but what I see now is..."

(This is your chance to witness yourself with love and clarity. Speak it.)

4. "One way I still carry that creative spark today is..."

(Through your work, your hobbies, your parenting, your style, your ideas—honor the thread that connects little you to current you.)

5. "I rise because..."

(Say it strong. Say it boldly. Say it like a mic drop.)

Optional:

Write this in your book:

"This chapter reminded me that joy is my birthright, and creativity is my rebellion."

Need support?

Scan the QR code to hear me guide you through this Reflect Ritual.

Let's rise together. You're not alone in this.

Morocco taught me color.

— Yves Saint Laurent

CHAPTER SIX

THE WORLD TOUR

Now, obviously, my superstar career didn't take off just yet, but that didn't mean I wasn't well-traveled. Oh, I traveled the world (kind of). Just... not in a private jet. Or on a glamorous tour bus. No, my "world tour" looked a little different. Every year, we traveled to Morocco or Tunisia.

Not in a quick two-to-four-hour flight kind of way. (Just to clarify—Tunisia was a two-hour flight, Morocco was four!)

But we didn't fly. Oh no. We did it the old-school way—the North African immigrant way.

No private jets. No glamorous tour buses.

Our "world tour" was a beat-up car packed to the brim, full of bags, snacks, siblings, cassette tapes, and prayers that the engine wouldn't overheat. No AC either.

We'd leave Germany and drive all the way through France and Spain. Hugging the highways that curved along the Mediterranean, we'd snake our way south. And back then, there weren't sleek highways everywhere, especially not in southern Spain. I'll never forget those mountain roads near Granada, narrow, winding, and terrifying. One wrong turn and you were looking at a cliff. No guardrails, just raw nature and white knuckles on the steering wheel. As a kid, I sat in the backseat gripping my little pillow like it had superpowers.

And no matter where we went—Morocco or Tunisia—at some point, we always had to face the ferry. If we were heading to Morocco, we'd wait in long lines of cars under the blazing Spanish sun, inching our way toward the ferry in Algeciras. If it was Tunisia, we'd drive to Genoa, Italy, and board the massive ferry that would carry us across the Mediterranean.

That part? That was its own kind of adventure.

Imagine hundreds of families just like ours, cars stuffed with luggage, people, food, gifts for relatives, and entire household items. Everyone sweating in the heat, windows rolled down, car engines off, and people wandering around waiting for their turn to load. The chaos was something else—horns, shouting in Arabic, kids running between cars, someone always looking for lost documents, someone else selling drinks from a cooler.

But once we were on board, it was a whole new world. The ferries were massive, like floating apartment buildings. We'd explore every corner, play games with other kids, trade snacks, peek over the railings to watch the waves, and try to spot dolphins. The adults relaxed, shared food, drank tea, and swapped stories in a hundred different dialects. It smelled like sea salt, diesel, sweat, and spices—and somehow, that mix meant home.

It was exhausting, chaotic, and at times, absolutely magical. That strange, beautiful feeling of being in between two worlds—European roads behind us, North Africa waiting just ahead.

Back then, I especially hated the car rides. The heat. The endless driving. The "Are we there yet?" that had no clear answer. The boredom. The cramped legs. The sunburned necks. The cassette tapes and Arabic classics my parents played way too loud. All we wanted was to listen to our own songs and fast-forward through time. But thank God for Walkmans, tangled headphones, and backpacks full of magazines and half-melted chocolate bars.

Now? Now I look back and realize how lucky we were.

Because my parents gave us something priceless: perspective.

We grew up in a first-world country, but every summer, we went to a third-world country. We saw different cultures, different foods, and different ways of life. We learned languages, we learned resilience, and most importantly, we learned gratitude.

Every year, it was like pressing pause on order, structure, and sparkling-clean sidewalks... and stepping into this wild, colorful, chaotic world that pulsed with life.

We played soccer barefoot in dusty streets with kids who didn't own cleats but had more joy than anyone I'd ever met. We used the old school toilets—you know, the ones where you have to squat all the way down, pray for balance, and hope your aim is good. (Western kids, don't try this at home.) No flush buttons. No toilet paper pyramids. Just you, gravity, and a bucket of water.

We visited families who lived in homes without running water, and yet they were always smiling, always singing. They didn't have much, but somehow they had everything. That joy? That fire? You could feel it in your bones.

My parents had worked so hard in Germany to build a beautiful house in both Morocco and Tunisia. But the idea of a vacation home? Ha. That house was never empty. It was packed—and I mean packed—with family. I grew up thinking it was totally normal to have your aunts, uncles, cousins, your mom's eight siblings, and your grandparents all living rent-free in your family's house.

And honestly? It kind of made sense. Leaving a house empty all year? That's just asking for someone to break in. So, yeah—let the whole clan move in. Safer. Louder. Crazier. And more fun.

Every summer, that house exploded with laughter, fights, chaos, and the smell of spices. Our aunts—many of them closer to us in age than to my mom—were like the older sisters we never had. They took us out, showed us life, and taught us everything we probably shouldn't have learned at that age. Street smarts. How to talk our way out of trouble. How to sneak out and still look innocent. (Sorry, Mama.)

They rewired our brains. They showed us another way to think, beyond rules and structure. They taught us how to hustle a little, how to adapt, how to read a room. One moment we were sipping mint tea, the next we were getting life lessons in survival, sass, and style.

Those summers shaped us. They made our minds complex and creative. We learned to mix the best of both worlds: the precision, order, and discipline of Germany, and the resilience, flair, and street savvy of North Africa.

And somehow, that mix? It made us magic.

But here's the strange part—no matter where we were, we were always kind of the outsiders. In Germany, we were the foreigners. And in Morocco and Tunisia, we were also the foreigners—the so-called rich foreigners.

And even though we weren't rich by any means in Germany, in North Africa, we were seen as privileged, admired, and treated with a kind of respect we didn't always feel back home. For once, it felt... good to be seen that way. To taste what it felt like to be the one with a little more, even just for the summer. It was a strange but powerful shift that stayed with me.

And through all the noise, the hustle, and the laughter, our family taught us the greatest lesson of all: that life isn't about what you have, but who you have. We learned that wealth isn't always measured in money. Sometimes, it's in the warmth of a kitchen full of people. In the stories passed down over mint tea. In the roots that remind you who you are and where you come from.

That kind of wealth shaped me more than I could ever explain.

It grounded me.

It gave me culture, pride, and perspective.

It showed me that even with three homes, three identities, and three different worlds...

I was whole.

And I am whole.

And—just to throw in a little truth nugget for the culture—I am what they call a third culture kid. You know the ones. Born in one country, raised in another, and shaped by a third (or more).

In my case?

Born in Germany. Raised with Moroccan and Tunisian culture. And now living in America.

So really, I'm not just a third culture kid—I'm a walking mosaic.

It means I've got more than one root system—and those roots twist into each other in the most beautiful, confusing, magical ways.

It means I'm fluent in blending in and standing out at the same time.

I'm always code-switching, culture-flipping, passport-juggling, and identity-mixing.

And guess what?

That's my superpower.

THE LESSON & REFLECT RITUAL

The Lesson

You don't have to pick just one culture, one box, or one version of home.

You are allowed to be complex. You are allowed to belong in many places—or none at all.

And still be whole.

The world may try to label you, but you get to define you.

Being raised between cultures doesn't mean you're confused.

It means you are layered, fluent, and unshakably grounded in something bigger.

You carry flavors, stories, and memories that stretch across borders.

That's not a burden. That's a gift.

REFLECT RITUAL – CHAPTER 6: The World Tour

"My roots are global. My identity is rich. My story is mine."

Your Tools:

• A quiet space

• A mirror

• Your phone (open voice memo or camera)

• 3 minutes of courage

Your Reflect Ritual (Say these out loud):

1. One way my cultural background shaped me is... I learned how to cook with flavor and soul, I speak a second language, or you were born and raised in the same town, but your family's traditions made you feel wonderfully unique.)

2. A time I felt like an outsider in my own home country was...(when someone asked, "But where are you really from?" , when your lunch smelled "too spicy" for the cafeteria, or simple the quiet ache of never fully fitting in.)

3. One part of my identity I've learned to love is...(your name, your hair, your accent, your "in-between-ness," your rituals, your roots.)

4. A gift I bring to the world because of my cultural roots is...(your storytelling, your ability to move between worlds, your deep empathy, your spices, your rhythm, your perspective.)

5. I rise because... my story is layered and real, I belong everywhere I go, I am not confused—I am complete.)

Optional:

Write this in your book:

"This chapter reminded me that I am allowed to be many things—and all of them are real."

Need support?

Scan the QR code to hear me guide
you through this Reflect Ritual.

Let's rise together. You're not alone
in this.

You can't stop the waves, but you can learn how to surf.

— Jon Kabat-Zinn

CHAPTER SEVEN

THE DAY I ALMOST DIED... AGAIN

It was the summer of 1992.

Hot. Loud. Magic. Morocco.

As always, my whole family had made the journey down from Germany for our annual summer in North Africa. That year, the heat wrapped around us like a thick blanket, the kind that made your skin glisten before 10 a.m. But we didn't care. We were where we belonged, back with our roots, our people, our laughter.

That day, we headed to the beach in Kenitra called Sidi Bou Ghaba. It wasn't our first beach day of the summer—we'd already been in Morocco for a couple of weeks, but this was one of those big, all-out family days. The kind that stays in your memory not because you knew something would happen, but because something did.

My mom, as always, went all out. You'd think we were planning a wedding reception by the ocean, not just a beach day. She packed real food, not "snacks"—actual lunch: meat, bread, salads, drinks, sweets. We had beach chairs, sunbrellas, folding tables, tablecloths, the whole setup. My aunts and uncles, maybe seven or eight of them, were all there, plus my parents, my older sister, my older brother, and all the cousins. That's how we rolled, big, loud, loving.

The air was filled with the sound of seagulls, kids laughing, the sizzling heat of the sun baking the sand, and the familiar chants of vendors roaming the beach.

"Limonade, limonade! Limonade Berda, Berda umberda!"

Men carried giant coolers full of icy soda, shouting over one another like it was a sport. Others balanced trays of sweets, chewing gum, candy, donuts, and ice cream. It was chaos, but it was the kind of chaos that made you feel alive.

We all went down to the water, my mom, some of her sisters, and me. My mom was in such a good mood. You could tell she was around her sisters, laughing that carefree laugh that only came out during these summers. The kind of joy that only happens when you return to the place where your soul exhales.

I held her hand as we walked in, the waves brushing against our legs. The Atlantic wasn't looking as wild that day, and I wasn't afraid.

Then I looked across the beach and saw my sister and my youngest aunt swimming farther down. They looked so cool. Younger. Freer. I thought to myself, I don't want to be with my mom and the older aunts, I want to be with them. They looked like they were having more fun.

So I made a decision.

No goodbye.

No plan.

Just the wild confidence of a young girl who couldn't even swim properly.

I let go of my mom's hand and began walking, confident, determined, to the other side of the beach. It didn't seem far. Just a little walk through the ocean, right?

But then, the ground started slipping beneath my feet. I stepped forward, and it got deeper. Then deeper again. It felt like stairs going down into the sea. Suddenly, I was in over my head, literally.

Then it happened.

A pull.

A twist.

A spinning.

A vortex. Like a watery tornado underneath the surface. A whirlpool.

I didn't have the words for it then. All I knew was that my body was caught in something stronger than me, spinning me like a wheel underwater.

I tried to swim up. I kicked and flailed and reached for air.

But each time I got close to the surface, a wave smashed over me, forcing me back under.

I gasped.

Choked.

Fought.

And then I started losing.

I felt the fight in me slipping. My little body was tired. I heard muffled screams. I saw sunbeams flickering through the water.

And then, this part is hard to describe; everything slowed down.

The panic turned to stillness.

My body stopped fighting.

And this eerie, terrifying peace washed over me.

I thought, this is it.

I'm dying.

This is how I go.

Then suddenly, a grip.

A hand grabbed my arm.

And yanked me out.

My head broke through the surface. And then the sounds came rushing in—the ocean, the screaming, the vendors yelling, the world. Life.

A guy who had been playing volleyball nearby had seen my mom screaming and asking for help. He saw me struggling and jumped in to save me. He pulled me out of that vortex like an angel sent mid-game.

When we got to the shore, I was disoriented. The first thing I saw was my mom.

Her face was streaked with tears and blood—she had scratched herself in the panic, running barefoot across the sand to reach me, thinking she was watching her baby drown.

Then my uncle, one of my favorites, ran up and started screaming at me.

Not hugging.

Not checking on me.

Screaming.

"Why would you do this? What were you thinking?!"

And in that moment, I didn't understand. I had almost died, and now I was being yelled at like I had broken a dish.

Now that I'm older, I know it came from fear. From trauma. From that old-school cultural conditioning that says when something bad happens, we yell so it never happens again.

But little me? I just felt ashamed.

I felt like I had done something wrong.

When all I had done was try to get to the fun side of the beach.

A little later that day, we packed up and left.

My mom was hugging me and silent, pale, shaking. The rest of the summer, she had horrible migraines and barely left her bed.

I bounced back quickly. Kids do that.

I went back to the beach within days. I didn't even think twice.

And that's the thing, I never lost my love for the water.

Even though that day tried to take it away.

I still love to swim. Pools are my preference, probably for that reason.

Give me a clear, still pool where I can see the bottom and not get pulled into the underworld, thank you very much.

But I still go to the ocean. I still swim. I still laugh in the water with my kids. I still let the salt touch my skin, and the sun dry it after.

Because no part of me wants to hand over my joy to fear.

Still, for years after that day, I had the same recurring nightmare.

A tsunami.

Always a tsunami.

Sometimes I was running. Sometimes I was watching the water come for me. Sometimes I was in a car and saw the ocean rise and spill onto the land like a monster unchained.

Even watching Aquaman triggered me. That scene where he drives along the coast and suddenly, BOOM—he looks out the window and sees the water coming—that giant wave about to swallow everything.

Every time I see something like that, even now, I instinctively gasp for air.

It's like my body still remembers.

For so many years, I didn't connect it to trauma.

I just thought I had weird dreams.

But now? Now I know better.

Especially coming from my culture, Mediterranean, Arabic—we believe deeply in dreams. We see them as messages, signs, warnings.

And I've always been a dream girl. I pay attention to what my subconscious tries to tell me at night. I listen.

Because now I know: A lot of our dreams are just unprocessed pain trying to be heard.

That tsunami dream was my trauma on repeat.

It wasn't just a bad memory. It was my body and soul replaying the moment I almost drowned—again and again—until I made peace with it.

And I'm still making peace with it.

Even today, I remind myself:

You're not little Sisi anymore.

You're not that tiny girl stuck in the ocean, flailing and gasping.

You're a grown woman. A mama. A protector.

You get to choose how far you go.

You get to feel into the day and say, "Hmm, the waves look wild, I think I'll stay close to shore today."

You are not helpless anymore.

You're responsible. You're wise. You can assess risk. You can keep your babies safe.

But most importantly, I tell myself:

You are allowed to enjoy the ocean again.

Just do it with respect.

With presence.

With awareness.

Because nature doesn't play, and you better not either.

And now, as a mother, I've made a vow:

I will not project my fear onto my children.

Yes, I'll teach them to respect the ocean.

Yes, I'll hold their hands and watch them closely.

Yes, I'll create the safest space possible for them to explore.

But I will not pass on the panic.

I want them to feel the magic, not just the danger.

Because that's how I try to raise them,

By building a safe environment around them... and then letting them play freely inside it.

That's what breaking cycles looks like.

That's what healing looks like.

That's what love looks like.

THE LESSON & REFLECT RITUAL

The Lesson

Your Fear Doesn't Get to Steal Your Joy, But It Does Deserve Your Respect

Some things will shake you so deeply, your body remembers what your mind tries to forget.

You might survive something and walk away smiling. But that doesn't mean it didn't scar you. That doesn't mean your heart didn't flinch every time you got too close to the edge again.

Trauma is sneaky like that. It lives in your dreams. In the way you flinch at a wave. In the nightmares, you keep brushing off.

But here's the thing:

Just because something tried to drown you doesn't mean you have to stay dry forever.

Yes, you have the right to be cautious.

Yes, you should respect the ocean, the wild, the moments that once knocked the wind out of you.

But you also deserve to laugh again.

To go back to the shore and dance in the waves—even if just ankle-deep.

And if you're a mama? You get to decide whether to pass on fear or freedom.

I choose freedom.

I teach my children to respect the ocean, to stay safe, but I don't let my trauma become their story.

I build them a safe world and let them discover it with joy.

Because they deserve to feel wonder, not just warning.

They deserve the joy the ocean still holds.

You're not that little girl anymore.

You're grown. You're wise. You're a mother now.

You know when the waves are too wild.

You know how to stay present and read the moment.

So honor your fear.

But don't let it cage you.

Your joy is still yours.

Your peace is still possible.

And your power?

It's not in avoiding the ocean forever.

It's in knowing how to walk back into it—eyes open, heart steady, grounded in your truth.

Because healing doesn't mean forgetting.

It means remembering—and still choosing to live.

Let's reflect.

You've earned this moment.

REFLECT RITUAL – CHAPTER 7 The Day I Almost Died... Again

"I Respect the Waves — But I Won't Let Them Own Me."

Your Tools:

• A quiet space

• A mirror

• Your phone (open voice memo or camera)

• 3 minutes of courage

Your Reflect Ritual (Say these out loud):

1. "One time in my life when I felt like I was drowning emotionally, mentally, or physically was..."

(Even if you didn't know it then—name it now. Bring light to it.)

2. "A fear I've carried with me longer than I realized is..."

(Was it a wave? A word? A moment? Say it loud.)

3. "A dream, scene, or image that keeps showing up in my sleep or thoughts is..."

(Your body and mind are talking to you. Listen to them.)

4. "What I now know is... I am not that little girl anymore because..."

(Speak to her gently. Tell her what she never got to hear.)

5. "I can choose joy again, even after fear, because today I know that ..."

(You're healing. You're aware. You're enough. Say it from your soul.)

Optional:

Write this in your book :

"This chapter reminded me that my fears are not flaws. They are echoes of moments I survived.

I don't have to silence them.

But I do get to decide how loud they speak."

Need support?

Scan the QR code to hear me guide you through this Reflect Ritual.

Let's rise together. You're not alone in this.

I believe in being strong when everything seems to be going wrong.

— Audrey Hepburn

Chapter Eight

THE COOL KID

(KIND OF)

After a rocky start—burn scars, bad teachers, and too many reasons to feel like an outsider—something finally began to shift. Fifth grade. Just when I thought school would always be a struggle, fifth grade showed up with a plot twist.

I was more confident. I had more friends. Life had changed a lot (probably because of the fight I had in fourth grade), and for the first time in forever, I didn't feel like the outsider. Our classes got mixed that year, which meant new faces, new energy, and honestly? It felt like someone had hit the refresh button. I was actually excited to go to school—mostly to socialize, let's be real—but still, it felt good.

But before I go on, I need to take you on a little detour so you understand the stage I was standing on. Let me explain the German school system for those of you thinking, "Wait, didn't she just talk about elementary school?"

So, here's how it works in Germany: from first to fourth grade, all kids go to the same type of elementary school. No sorting, no pressure, just tiny humans trying to survive snack time and learn to write their names in cursive. But after fourth grade? Boom. That's when the system starts making decisions for you.

Based on your grades, teachers recommend which school you go to next. The top students, the ones with good grades, neat handwriting, and likely parents who read Einstein quotes over breakfast, get sent to Gymnasium. That's the elite path. The university-bound crowd. The future lawyers, doctors, and people who know how to use semicolons correctly.

Then there's Hauptschule. That's where the other kids go.

Guess where I landed?

Yep. Hauptschule.

And you know what? At first, it actually felt... kinda cool.

Most of the "super smart" kids—the ones who always raised their hands, who have made me feel unseen, and whose parents probably hired tutors in kindergarten—were gone. They marched off to Gymnasium like little academic soldiers. And those of us left behind? We were mostly kids with immigrant parents—Gastarbeiterkinder—plus a few German kids who hadn't quite made the cut either. For the first time, I wasn't the odd one out anymore. I was just one of the crowd. It was... freeing.

I even started to like school. Not for the academics, let's not get crazy. But for the vibe, the friendships, the laughs during breaks, and the drama in the hallways. It was fun.

The best part? My best friend Mona, who also happened to live one floor below me in our apartment building, was still in my class. And a bunch of other kids I liked were too. Some of them would go on to become lifelong friends. Fifth grade felt like the beginning of something fresh. I wasn't the invisible, lonely girl anymore. I was in. I belonged.

But before I let you get too cozy in this fifth-grade glow-up, let me rewind for a sec. Because there's something that's always haunted me.

Back when I was supposed to start kindergarten, something went wrong. Either my parents messed up to enroll me in time, or the system did—honestly, I don't even know. But the result? I didn't get into the same kindergarten as most of the other kids from my neighborhood. And that small mistake had consequences.

By the time we got to elementary school, everyone already knew each other. They had their little cliques, their inside jokes from finger-painting days, their "remember when" stories—and I was just... there. Technically, I was with them. But emotionally? I was always playing catch-up. I didn't talk about it much, but the feeling of being an outsider never really left me.

And now... let's talk about him.

Yes, him. There was this one boy. I'd known him since first grade. He wasn't in my class, just in the same grade with a different teacher. And listen, I don't care how many years go by—this boy will always have a special little corner in my heart.

Why? Because—believe it or not—he liked me.

Like... a real, honest-to-God schoolboy crush. And this wasn't just any boy. No, no. This was the most popular boy in the entire school. The one every girl had a crush on. The one with the perfect hair and the effortlessly cool vibe. And out of all the girls, there were a few moments in time when he liked me.

I could hardly believe it.

Because let's be real: I didn't think much of myself back then. I had wild, frizzy hair, chocolate brown skin in a sea of pale, and I was a burn survivor. I thought I was awkward, unpopular, and definitely not the type of girl the popular boy crushed on. But knowing that he liked me—even for a little while? That was a game-changer. It made me feel seen. Like, really seen. And I've never forgotten that.

By fifth grade, we were finally in the same class. We became good friends. And as the years passed? Sisi went from awkward and overlooked to... well, kinda cool.

Yep. Somehow, in Hauptschule, I became somebody. I even became the school president. I don't want to brag, but that's how cool I became.

I had lots of friends. I felt confident. I wasn't about that mean-girl life either. I used my popularity to bring people in, especially the ones who felt left out. I remembered what it felt like to be excluded, so I tried to be the kind of friend I always wished I had.

But then... something started happening.

Little by little, my friends began leaving Hauptschule. Some moved on to Realschule, which is kind of the second-best school you can go to. A few even made the leap to Gymnasium. And guess what? My best friend Mona, the one who lived just downstairs, left too.

And every time someone left, it felt like another message: "They're moving up. You're staying behind."

Socially? I was still thriving. My crew was strong, and even the ones who left for other schools stayed close. We still met up, hung out, and shared laughs like nothing had changed.

But emotionally? Oh, it hit hard. With every friend who moved on, the voice in my head got louder:

You're not smart enough. You'll never be smart enough.

THE LESSON & REFLECT RITUAL

The Lesson

Being liked is not the same as believing in yourself.

You can be loved, admired, even popular—and still secretly feel unworthy.

But the truth is: your brilliance is not up for debate. You don't have to prove you're smart.

You just have to stop hiding from your own light.

Let's get practical.

It's time to reflect and rise.

REFLECT RITUAL – CHAPTER 8: The Cool Kid... Kind Of

"I Belong—Even When I Doubt It"

Your Tools:

• A quiet space

• A mirror

• Your phone (open voice memo or camera)

• 3 minutes of courage

Your Reflect Ritual (Say these out loud):

1. "A time I felt seen, but still unsure of myself was…"

(Maybe it was school. A relationship. A leadership role. Speak the moment.)

2. "The lie I started to believe about myself was…" I'm not smart enough. I'll never catch up. I don't deserve this.)

3."What I now know is…"

(Rewrite that story. Speak your real truth. Loud. Proud. From the gut.)

4. "What I would say to the version of me who wanted to quit is…"

(Show her grace. Then show her the way forward.)

5. "I rise because…"

(Let this line land like a promise. Let it echo.)

Optional:

Write this in your book:

"This chapter reminded me that true confidence means..."

Need support?

Scan the QR code to hear me guide
you through this Reflect Ritual.

Let's shake off shame and say what's
true, together.

It always seems impossible until it's done.

— Nelson Mandela

CHAPTER NINE

THE CHEERLEADER GERMANY NEVER ASKED FOR

When I was in sixth grade, I was basically a walking, talking, European version of an American Dream enthusiast. No question—I was obsessed. I loved everything about America. The cheerleaders, the high school football games, the beautiful suburban houses with white picket fences. In my head, my future was set. I was going to grow up in the U.S., become a cheerleader, live in a picture-perfect home with my parents and siblings, and—of course—date a dreamy football player. Obviously, he would carry my books down the hallway, and I would wear his oversized football jacket, because that's what all the movies promised.

To make things even more extra, I wasn't just into the America of now—oh no, I was all about the old school America. The 50s, the 60s, the oldies but goldies music. My sister and I would sing out songs like we were the next big thing in rock 'n' roll, even though we were just two young Arabic girls in Germany who couldn't even drive yet.

But here's the problem with being an American cheerleader in Germany in the 90s: nobody knew what cheerleading even was. The concept was so foreign to my teachers.

Our school didn't have American football. We had soccer (Fussball). And even our school's soccer team wasn't a real soccer team—it was just a bunch of classmates kicking a ball around, hoping to score and impress their crushes. But did that stop me? Absolutely not.

One day, I marched up to my sports teacher, full of confidence, dreams, and just enough audacity to be a problem, and said, "We need a cheerleading team."

She looked at me like I had just asked her to let me bring a pet lion to school. "Cheerleader? What is cheerleading? No, Sisi. You cannot be doing this. Leave me alone."

Excuse me? No was simply not in my vocabulary when it came to my cheerleading dreams. So, naturally, I did what any determined future cheer captain would do: I asked her again. And again. And again.

Week after week, I was in her face, pushing, pleading, pitching my grand idea. I was relentless. Until one day, she finally had enough.

She turned to me, sighed dramatically, and said, "Fine, Sisi. You get five minutes. Get out of my face. Do whatever you want."

Five minutes! Did I take it? Oh, you bet I did! Because five minutes is better than zero minutes, and I was about to make the most of them.

I ran with it. I went to the stores, bought supplies, I handcrafted pom-poms—yes, DIY before Pinterest made it cool. I recruited a squad of girls who were just crazy enough to trust me, choreographed a routine, found the perfect outfits, and turned that tiny sliver of opportunity into a full-blown moment.

And when game day came, there we were, our little, slightly confused cheer squad, shaking our handmade pom-poms and yelling out cheers for a soccer team that actually cared more than we thought they would, and the rest of the school thought that it was the coolest thing ever. It was a very proud moment. I remember being so happy that I stayed persistent. Because for once, I wasn't waiting for someone to give me a chance, I gave one to myself.

THE LESSON & REFLECT RITUAL

The Lesson

Your dream doesn't need a blueprint or approval. It needs you.

You don't have to wait for someone to create the space. You are the space.

Sometimes the world doesn't catch up to your vision until you've already made it real—and that's okay.

Lead anyway.

Let's get practical.

It's time to reflect and rise.

REFLECT RITUAL – CHAPTER 9: The Cheerleader That Germany Never Asked For

"I Don't Wait for Permission to Shine"

Your Tools:

• A quiet space

• A mirror

• Your phone (open voice memo or camera)

• 3 minutes of courage

Your Reflect Ritual (Say these out loud):

1."A time I had a vision no one else understood was…"

(It could be a passion, an idea, or a dream they thought was "too much." Speak it out loud.)

2. "The part of me that pushed forward anyway was..."

(What kicked in? Courage? Spite? Joy? Name the fire that moved you forward.)

3. "Looking back, I'm proud that ..."

(Say it. Honor it. Take up space in your own win.)

4. "Today, when people doubt me, I remind myself that..."

(Give yourself the pep talk. Be your own hype squad.)

5. "I rise because..."

(Let it land like the stomp at the end of a cheer. Final. Fierce. Yours.)

Optional:

Write this in your book:

"This chapter reminded me that my vision is..."

Need support?

Scan the QR code to hear me guide
you through this Reflect Ritual.

No one's cheering louder for you
than me—let's rise.

Tear down that wall of fear.

— Sisi Surgant

CHAPTER TEN

1998: THE DAY I ALMOST PEED MYSELF IN FRONT OF THOUSANDS

I was fourteen, full of dreams, full of excitement, and—let's be real—full of way too much teenage confidence. That year, my sister and I were beyond thrilled to go to a festival in Munich called Happy Family. And let me tell you, this festival was the place to be. It had everything—music, fun, people from everywhere, and a big stage where actual stars performed.

And this year? The big act was Basis. Now, if you don't remember them, don't worry, most people don't. They were huge in 1998 in Germany at least, but like a lot of 90s bands, they vanished quicker than a Tamagotchi left unattended. But at that moment, they were the real deal, and we were pumped.

My sister and I, along with our crew of girlfriends, were ready for a day of music, fun, and just being young and fabulous. There was even a little basketball tournament happening, which was great for whoever cared, but my focus was on the stage. You see, back then, I was big into singing and rapping. Like, really into it.

I thought I was just one talent scout away from being discovered.

And then, I made the mistake, or maybe the not mistake, of speaking my thoughts out loud. "Oh, I'd love to sing here," I muttered, mostly to myself.

Now, let's talk about my sister for a second. She has zero hesitation when it comes to supporting me. Where most people would say, "Oh, that's nice," and move on, my sister? She makes things happen. And by makes things happen, I mean she went straight to the host of the event, told them her little sister wanted to sing, and just like that, I was signed up.

The host was like, "Sure, she can sing."

And I was like: Excuse me, what?

I could feel my soul trying to escape my body. Like, how was this happening? Who gave my sister the right to throw me into a potential public humiliation disaster? But before I could protest, I was in it.

So there I was, about to sing in front of a massive crowd, nerves doing cartwheels in my stomach, when someone suddenly grabbed my arm and whispered, "Come with me."

Next thing I knew, they whisked me backstage—not to warm up or prep for my performance—but to judge a basketball dunking competition. Yes, you read that right. Judge. A. Basketball. Performance. I still don't know how all of this happened, but there I was. Supposedly an insider.

They handed me a clipboard like I was some kind of expert and sat me down courtside, right next to this tall, cool-looking guy. At this point, I'm still trying to figure out why people are chasing a ball like it's the last piece of bread on Earth, and I'm over here like... Why am I here? What's happening?

Now listen, I knew a little bit about basketball. I wasn't totally clueless—I understood the basics: throw the ball in the hoop, try not to foul, run fast. But enough to judge a full tournament? Absolutely not. And yet there I was, clipboard in hand, legs crossed, nodding like I knew what was going on. Spoiler: I didn't.

And then... here's the kicker. Sitting right next to me—cool as ever—was none other than Magic Johnson.

Yes. *The* Magic Johnson.

Now, did I realize that in the moment? Nope. Not even a little bit. I had heard the name before, sure, but the face? Completely unregistered. I was fifteen, sitting there clueless, thinking he was just some very tall basketball guy with a very confident vibe.

So what did I do?

I cheated.

Yup. Every time he wrote something on his judging sheet, I casually glanced over and copied the exact same thing. Word for word. I figured, whoever this guy was, he clearly looked like he knew what he was doing—and I definitely didn't. And honestly? Flawless strategy. No notes.

But enough about that.

Let's get back to the real drama: my performance.

Finally, it was my turn. They called my name. Thousands of people were watching. My legs felt like pudding, my heart was pounding, and I thought, "Yup, this is it. This is where I die."

But I walked up there. And I sang.

And of course, I sang I Wanna Be Down by Brandy. Because, obviously, that was my song. It had become an inside joke at that point—if I was gonna sing, you knew it was gonna be Brandy.

And guess what? People loved it.

I remember the crowd cheering, clapping, and hyping me up. And that feeling—the mix of terror, adrenaline, and pure magic—was something I would never forget.

Looking back, I think about how many times we stop ourselves from doing things because of fear. We build up this massive wall of fear brick by brick, year after year. People, teachers, family—even ourselves—we all contribute to it. We convince ourselves that the world is too scary, that we aren't good enough, that we'll fail.

But if you tear that wall of fear down, there is magic on the other side. That day, my sister pushed me through a door I was too scared to open myself. And I'm so glad she did. (Love you, sis!)

Because even if my hands were shaking, even if I almost peed myself, even if my voice wobbled at the beginning, and probably wasn't even the best, I did it.

And it was worth it.

Ever since that day, I have taken every opportunity to sing randomly at all kinds of events.

So, if you have a dream, if you have a moment where you can step up and take a shot, please do it. The fear is temporary. The regret of not trying? That lasts forever.

THE LESSON & REFLECT RITUAL

The Lesson

Fear will always show up, but courage is doing it anyway.

That wobbly voice? That racing heart? That is the sound of you stretching into who you're becoming.

Do it scared. Do it shaking. But do it. Because the regret of playing small lasts way longer than the fear of showing up big.

Let's get practical.

It's time to reflect and rise.

REFLECT RITUAL – CHAPTER 10: The Day I Almost Peed Myself

"Fear Doesn't Get to Run the Show"

Your Tools:

• A quiet space

• A mirror

• Your phone (open voice memo or camera)

• 3 minutes of courage

Your Reflect Ritual (Say these out loud):

1. "A time I almost said no out of fear was…"

(Think of that one thing you wanted—on stage, at work, in love—but almost ran from. Name it.)

2. "What I was most afraid of in that moment was…"

(Failure? Judgment? Looking silly? Speak it out loud. No shame.)

3. "But when I did it anyway, I felt…"

(Even if it was messy or imperfect—what did showing up give you?)

4. "Now I know that fear is…"

(A liar? A signpost? Temporary? Name what fear really is—not what it pretends to be.)

5. "I rise because…"

(Say it like you're holding a mic. Like your voice matters. Because it does.)

Optional:

Write this in your book:

"This chapter reminded me that courage means..."

Need support?

Scan the QR code to hear me guide you through this Reflect Ritual.

We're walking through fear together. Let's rise.

The most courageous act is still to think for yourself.

— Coco Chanel

CHAPTER ELEVEN

LOVE, LESSONS, AND A CAR RIDE IN MOROCCO

As I mentioned before, every summer, like clockwork, we packed our bags and headed to Morocco. Sometimes we'd make it to Tunisia too, but mostly, our time was spent in Morocco. And listen, those summers were long. We're talking six to eight weeks of heat, family, tradition, and—depending on my mood—either the best time ever or the slowest countdown to school reopening.

See, as I got older, I really started loving school—not for studying (let's not be irrational), but I loved it because of my friends and socializing (I guess that's where my love for socializing started).

I missed them. I wanted to be back. But at the same time, Morocco was filled with memories, lessons, and experiences that shaped me in ways I didn't even realize back then.

One of the most vivid memories I have is a quiet, almost ordinary moment that, looking back, held so much weight. I was sitting in a car with my favorite aunt—my absolute favorite. She wasn't just an aunt to me; she was like a second mom. The way she loved and cared for me—I always felt like I was her extra child.

That night, we were parked in the dark, just waiting while her husband ran an errand. The air felt still, the streetlights casting shadows, and then, out of nowhere, she turned to me and dropped a truth bomb I did not ask for.

"Sisi, remember this for your life, you will never marry your big love. You will never marry the person you love the most. Life just doesn't work that way. You will settle."

Now, I was young, but I wasn't that young. And I wasn't about to take this as fact. My brain instantly went, Uh-uh, nope, not me. I didn't say anything at the moment, but inside? Oh, I was having a full romantic rebellion.

Because here's the thing, I have always, always been a love believer. A hopeless romantic. A love hyper. I love, love. I love seeing people in love, setting people up, talking about love, experiencing love, all of it. And I refused to accept the idea that love wasn't going to be the big, passionate, real thing I dreamed of. My name actually means Cupid, *hello!*

I know now that she wasn't trying to hurt me. That was her reality. Maybe that's how her life turned out. Maybe she settled. Maybe she believed that was just the way it had to be. And it breaks my heart that someone so full of love, so romantic at heart, had accepted that love wasn't for her in the way she dreamed.

But guess what? That was her story, not mine.

And spoiler alert: My life turned out completely different.

I married the love of my life. The kind of love that people write books and songs about. The kind of love that is perfect in itself, and so real, deep, and everything I ever hoped for. But okay, okay enough about my dreamboat of a husband... for now. I promise I will gush more about him and our love story a little later in the book. Spoiler alert: it gets a whole chapter. Because, well, he's just that good.

And if I had believed her words that night? If I had let that idea creep into my head, shaping my expectations? Maybe I wouldn't have fought for real love. Maybe I would've settled.

So here's what I want you to take from this:

Don't let someone else's pain become your blueprint. Rewrite the ending. Choose love, even if no one around you ever dared to.

THE LESSON & REFLECT RITUAL

The Lesson

Someone else's heartbreak is not your destiny.

You can honor where they came from and still choose a different path.

You don't have to repeat pain just because it's familiar.

You get to believe in love. You get to receive it. And you get to keep it.

Let's get practical.

It's time to reflect and rise.

REFLECT RITUAL – CHAPTER 11: Love, Lessons, and a Car Ride in Morocco

"I Choose Love—Even If They Didn't"

Your Tools:

• A quiet space

• A mirror

• Your phone (open voice memo or camera)

• 3 minutes of courage

Your Reflect Ritual (Say these out loud):

1. "A belief about love that was passed down to me was..."

(Maybe it was about settling. About sacrifice. About not deserving. Name it.)

2. "How that belief shaped me, even if I didn't realize it at that time..."

(Speak the truth. Did it hold you back? Make you afraid to ask for more?)

3. "But now I know that love can look like..."

(Paint your own picture. What does real, healthy, big love look like to you?)

4. "What I want my future (or current) love story to be built on is..."

(Trust? Values? Joy? Passion? Respect? Speak the foundation you're claiming.)

5. "I rise because..."

(Wrap it in truth. In worth. In love that starts with you.)

Optional:

Write this in your book:

"This chapter reminded me that I get to define love as...

Need support?

Scan the QR code to hear me guide
you through this Reflect Ritual.

Because love—real love—starts with
choosing you.

She remembered who she was, and the game changed.

— Lalah Delia

CHAPTER TWELVE

THE QUITTER WHO ACCIDENTALLY BECAME AN OVERACHIEVER

Let's talk about quitting. Not the dramatic, movie-style quitting where someone throws papers in the air, storms out, and delivers an I'm too good for this place speech. No, I'm talking about my personal specialty, quitting before even starting.

I was a professional quitter.

I had a solid, foolproof, can't-fail strategy: if you never take the exam, you never fail. Genius, right? Who needs the humiliation of proving they're dumb when you can just avoid it altogether? And deep down, that's exactly what I believed: I was dumb. People told me this in different ways since childhood. Family, teachers, even some friends, sometimes as a joke (we have a German saying:

behind every joke is a little bit of truth). But you know what happens when you hear something enough? Yep, you believe it.

So, my way of winning was simple: just don't try.

My shining moment? Ninth grade. Final exams.

This was the moment that determined our future. No pressure, right?

And here's the truth: I had no idea how to study. Literally—no clue. No one had ever taught me how. My immigrant parents couldn't help with school stuff, and I was too embarrassed to ask anyone else.

So, what did I do? I winged it. Like a true disaster queen.

And guess what? I failed.

Of course, I failed. I didn't even know what I was doing.

But what made it worse—what made it burn—was that by then, I was actually the girlfriend of the most popular boy in school. Yep, him again. And even though he was in my class and probably knew I wasn't exactly an academic star, something about that moment—failing that big, important test—felt like the final proof that I was officially dumb. I was mortified. Deep in my bones. I couldn't stop thinking: He's going to find out who I really am... and he's going to be embarrassed to be with me.

I was humiliated. Devastated. So ashamed that I made a dramatic decision, I'll repeat the whole year. Maybe with a fresh start, I'd finally figure it out.

Spoiler alert: I didn't.

I still didn't study. I still didn't know how. And when the next exam rolled around? I panicked.

So, what did I do?

I skipped it. Just didn't show up.

Automatic fail.

And here's where Sisi's twisted genius kicked in. I came up with what I thought was the perfect survival strategy: If I never try, I can never fail. See? Brilliant, right?

Because in my mind, it was better for people to think I was lazy than to think I was stupid. If I didn't show up, they couldn't say, "Wow, Sisi failed." They'd just think, "Oh, Sisi didn't even try." And for some reason, that felt easier to carry.

So that's what I did. Over and over again. I quit before I had the chance to fail. I backed out before I had to prove myself. It felt safer.

And that's how I left ninth grade. Still believing I wasn't smart enough. Still carrying that lie like it was carved in stone.

But life? Life had other plans for me.

Somehow, despite my elite-level quitting record, I still managed
to land incredible jobs—like, jaw-droppingly good ones. I worked
as a makeup artist for none other than Yves Saint Laurent, my
absolute idol, and traveled all across Germany—north, south, east,
and west—armed with a company car, a company credit card, hotel
rooms paid for, food paid for, and a serious sense of badassery. I
wasn't just doing makeup—I was embodying the art of transformation. And I got a true taste of what real fashion is all about.
That's what I learned from Yves Saint Laurent.

I went on to manage an entire boutique in fashion for Filippa
K, where I didn't just sell clothes—I created experiences. I styled
clients, built relationships, organized unforgettable fashion events,
and made the store feel like a runway dream. Later, I joined Calvin
Klein and strutted through the fashion world like I had a PhD in
fabulousness. People constantly assumed I had a high-level degree.
And every time they did, I felt this weird cocktail of pride—look at
me, fooling them!—and shame, oh no, now they'll know I'm just
winging it.

But then, as if the universe wanted to shake things up with its
signature twisted sense of humor, it placed the right boss in my
path. While I was managing a store for a Swedish fashion brand,
this boss casually dropped a life-altering offer: "Anyone working

here can study for a degree in retail if they want."And something in me just clicked.

Maybe it was the way people kept assuming I was qualified for things I wasn't. Maybe it was the quiet, nagging feeling that maybe I wasn't as dumb as I thought. Maybe I was just tired of running from myself.

Whatever it was, I signed up.

Not just me, my sister too. We were both running different store locations, so we figured, why not do it together? And what normally takes people three years, we crammed into three months of intense studying. And guess what? We killed it. Passed with flying colors.

That was my first little whisper of, Wait... am I actually smart?

And once that door cracked open? Oh, I kicked it wide open.

With my newfound confidence, I thought, Why stop here? So I signed up for another school to get a mid-level degree, the kind that put me one step closer to a university path. It was a year-long program, and I was the nerdiest student there.

I sat in the front row.

I asked every question possible.

I never skipped a day.

I never skipped my homework.

I discovered YouTube tutorials (I mean, why did no one ever tell me about these before?).

Can you guys even believe this?

And then—out of nowhere—something burst open inside me. For the first time in my life, I saw the truth: I wasn't dumb. I had never been dumb. I had just never been taught how to learn. Nobody had shown me how my brain worked, how I needed to be guided differently. All those years of thinking I was the problem, when really, the system had never met me where I was.

And just when I thought I had uncovered the biggest twist... an even bigger one came. Turns out—I was good at art. Art! Me, the girl who used to think drawing a stick figure was reaching the edge of her abilities. I still remember holding that pencil in my hand and seeing a shape come alive on the paper. It wasn't just decent—it was moving. And I didn't just like it, I loved it. I fell in love with the colors, the textures, the chaos, and the emotion of Expressionismus. It felt like I had found a hidden language that my soul had always spoken but never had the tools to express.

Suddenly, I was painting, drawing, creating, and thriving. For the first time, I wasn't surviving school—I was excelling. I finished the program with an A+ in art, and not just that... I found myself seen.

Recognized. My creativity wasn't just a fluke—it was a gift I never knew I had.

My brain was exploding. Who even am I?

Then came the ultimate challenge. Could I actually go back and get my full Gymnasium degree? You know—the one that opens the door to university. The one that belongs to the "smart kids." It was a long, hard road, and every step tested the version of me I had grown into. But I did it. I passed.

And then—just because I could—I took it even further. I applied to university. University. Can you even believe that? Me? The girl who thought quitting was the only way to survive? The girl who ran from failure before it could find her? The girl who once believed she wasn't good enough for anything?

I became someone I never believed I could be: the girl who stayed, who tried, who won.

I studied Business, Business Law, Business Ecology, and Human Resources, because years ago, when I worked for YSL and visited their headquarters in Munich, I saw all these powerful, stylish women in suits working at a beautiful, high-end office building. I remember thinking, "Wow, I want to work here," and so I asked one of the ladies, "How do I get a job here?" And she casually said, "Oh, you'd need a business degree."

At the time, I laughed internally. Yeah, right. Like that's ever happening.

And then, years later, life came full circle.

I got my degrees. I studied in Germany. Close to Munich. In Bavaria. And if you know anything about the German education system, you know—it's no joke. Germany is already known for being rigorous, but Bavaria? That's a whole different level. It's the hardest region in the entire country to earn a degree. And somehow, that's exactly where I did it. I got my university degree in the heart of Bavaria—and yes, that's something I carry with quiet pride. Because it wasn't just about getting through school. It was about doing it in the most demanding place possible, in a system not built for girls like me, and still making it all the way.

I was the first in my entire family to walk the halls of a university. The first to sit in lecture rooms with books piled high, deadlines looming, and dreams whispering that maybe, just maybe, I belonged. And that... was a really big deal.

I remember my dad's face. The way it lit up, not just with joy, but with something deeper. With pride. With awe. With this quiet, stunned wonder that his daughter—he, a man who came to a new country carrying more responsibility than language—had a child who earned a university degree in Germany.

He told everyone. I mean everyone. Doctors, neighbors, random people in waiting rooms. "My daughter has a degree." He would say it with this smile that was bigger than him. He would repeat it, like he needed to hear it again just to believe it. And each time, my heart swelled and broke a little too—because I saw how much it meant to him. How much it healed something in him. It wasn't just my dream that came true. It was his, too.

Where I grew up, even locals didn't often go to university. So for a girl like me, in a place like that, with a background like mine, it was almost unheard of. And yet, I did it. For him. For me. For all the girls who were told to aim lower.

And somewhere along the way, I realized something: I didn't become an overachiever because I was in love with achievements. I became an overachiever because I learned to hate quitting more than I feared failing.

And let me tell you—if I, a pro-level quitter, a master of self-sabotage, the girl who once believed she wasn't good enough for anything, can rise from that and become a university graduate... then you, my love, can absolutely do whatever it is you're scared of. Because failure? That's not the real enemy. Not trying is.

THE LESSON & REFLECT RITUAL

The Lesson

Quitting might feel safe, but it steals your potential. The only way to know what you're truly capable of is to show up and try.

Find help. Always ask for help. If you don't know how to do something, find a way to learn. Seek out the knowledge, the skills, and the guidance you need. Find a coach. Find a teacher. Find a tutor. Find a mentor. There is always someone out there who can help you achieve your goal; you just have to be willing to ask and take the first step.

Let's get practical.

It's time to reflect and rise.

REFLECT RITUAL – CHAPTER 12: The Quitter Who Accidentally Became an Overachiever

"I Was Never the Problem—The System Just Didn't See Me"

Your Tools:

• A quiet space

• A mirror

• Your phone (open voice memo or camera)

• 3 minutes of courage

Your Reflect Ritual (Say these out loud):

1. "A belief about myself that made me stop before I even started was..."

(Maybe it was about not being smart enough, not belonging, or always messing things up. Name it.)

2. "That belief held me back by..."

(Speak the truth. Did it make you quit too soon? Did it keep you small? Did it stop you from even trying?)

3. "But now I know that what I really needed was..."

(a different way of learning? More support? Someone to believe in you? Say what would've made a difference.)

4. "One thing I'm proud I didn't quit on is..."

(Brag on yourself. This is your celebration moment. Big or small—it counts.)

5. "I rise because..."

(Wrap it in truth. In resilience. In the unshakable fire of a woman who came back stronger.)

Optional:

Write this in your book:

"This chapter reminded me that I am allowed to rewrite the story I once believed about myself."

Need support?

Scan the QR code to hear me guide you through this Reflect Ritual.

Because being a late bloomer doesn't mean you're behind—

It means you bloom on your own terms.

Why do you stay in prison when the door is so wide open?

— Rumi

Chapter Thirteen

THE MOMENT I GAMBLED ON MYSELF AND WON

Let's take a moment. Seriously. Just a small pause to acknowledge the absolute miracle that is me in university.

Me. Sisi. In university.

I mean, excuse me, who even am I? Somebody hold my degree while I dance in this glow-up moment. I was the first in my entire family to make it this far. And remember that German system I told you about? Yeah, getting into university is not a casual, "Let me just apply and see what happens" kind of situation. Oh no, you're sorted out at age ten into categories that basically determine if you're "university material" or not. And let's just say, I was not sorted into the winning team.

But guess what? Here I was. Defying all odds.

My family was over the moon. My parents were so proud. My siblings were cheering me on. By all accounts, this should have been the happiest time of my life. But instead? It was one of my darkest.

Why? Because of one little detail. I was stuck in a soul-sucking, confidence-crushing, energy-draining relationship with a narcissist.

Now, let me clarify, I didn't just wake up one day and say, You know what would be fun? A deeply toxic relationship! No, no. It happened gradually, sneakily, in a way that only makes sense in hindsight.

Before this disaster, I was engaged to someone I truly, deeply loved. It was the kind of relationship people envy: healthy, happy, full of laughter, and mutual respect. We were best friends, teammates, in every way... or so it seemed. I adored him, and he adored me. When people looked at us, they said, "You two are forever." And for a long time, I believed them. I wanted to believe them.

But deep down, in the quiet moments, I knew something I didn't want to admit. He didn't really want to get married. Not truly. Not ever. We had different visions for life—I was more traditional, dreaming of a wedding, a family, little feet running through a sunlit home. But he was a free spirit, wild and beautiful, and convinced that marriage was a cage and fatherhood a concept that just didn't fit him.

And that crushed me. Not all at once, but slowly, year after year, as I stayed, hoping something might change. When he finally proposed, because he thought he had to. I of course said yes, but the truth is... I was already grieving. Because I knew that wasn't the love story I wanted to tell my future children. I couldn't bear the thought of one day explaining, "Well, I kind of had to convince your dad to marry me." That's not how my romantic heart works. That's not the kind of story I dreamed of building a life on.

So with a shattered heart, I walked away. After five and a half years together, and even more years of friendship, I let go of a man I loved—because loving him wasn't enough. It was one of the hardest, most soul-splitting decisions I've ever made. I was devastated. I felt hollow. I felt like I had just let go of my entire future.

I was so heartbroken I could barely move. Frozen in that grief. Lost.

And then, into that stillness, he waltzed in—literally waltzed, because he was Austrian. *Mr. Everybody-Loves-Him.* Charming? Check. Good-looking? Check. Financially stable? Check. Successful? Check. The biggest crush on me? Check.

He checked every damn box.

And when he proposed after just three months—yes, after three months of knowing me—I said yes.

Why? Honestly, I'm still not sure. Maybe it was my bruised ego whispering, "Look how fast this man wants to marry you," after spending years with someone who never really did. Maybe it was because the proposal happened on top of a cliff in Mallorca, and my survival instincts kicked in. (Say yes, or he pushes you off—joking! Halfway.)

Whatever it was, I said yes.

And I regretted it almost immediately.

Because, as it turns out, that man? That beautiful, successful, charming man?

He was the human version of a slow, painful migraine.

Manipulative. Controlling. Gaslighting at a professional level. He made me feel small, old, and trapped. He planned back-to-back vacations so I couldn't leave him. He convinced me that, at thirty years old, I was "too old" to find happiness elsewhere. He worked overtime to make sure I felt unwanted, unworthy, and powerless.

And for some reason, I stayed. Maybe because a small part of me believed him when he said I was too old to start over. Or maybe I was still carrying the weight of my last heartbreak—too frozen, too shocked, too tired to face another ending. It just felt easier to stay than to stand up and leave. And deep down, I wondered... what if he really was the best I could do? I truly believe there are people who bring out the best in you, and there are others who absolutely bring out the worst in you. And the latter happened to me.

I wasn't myself. I gained weight, lost my spark, and my confidence shrank into something I barely recognized. Even my friends noticed.

"Why do you talk to him like he's your teacher?" someone asked.

And I hated that. I hated that they were right. I hated myself for allowing it.

I don't know if you've ever been in a relationship where you know you're being manipulated—but somehow, you stay anyway.
It's like your brain keeps whispering, I'll leave soon. I just need a little more time. But that time never comes. And the longer you stay, the smaller you become. The moment that finally shook me was so simple—so innocent, really.

I had plans to pick up my nephew from school. He's my absolute heart—the boy I love like my own son. My fiancé was at work that day, which meant I had a rare window to do something that made me happy. All I wanted was to spend time with the one person who always lit up my world. But I knew my fiancé wouldn't be okay with that. If he wasn't involved, it didn't matter to him. If he wasn't around, I was supposed to stay still. Wait. Be quiet.

So I lied. I told him I was going grocery shopping. But really? I was picking up my nephew. And the second the lie left my mouth, I froze. I was lying about something so pure—just to avoid conflict with a man who claimed to love me. That was the moment I knew: I couldn't live like this. I couldn't live in fear of being me.

And then, the universe handed me an escape route.

I was in my penultimate semester at university, and for as long as I could remember, I had dreamed of studying abroad—specifically in America. Ever since I was a little girl, wide-eyed and obsessed with everything American—from the fashion and the freedom, to the idea that anything could happen there—I had imagined myself walking through a campus somewhere in the U.S., clutching books, sipping coffee from a red cup, and living the life I had only seen in movies. As you already know from earlier in this book, my obsession with America ran deep. What I couldn't admit out loud was, I never truly believed it would happen for me. How could it? I didn't have the kind of school education or background that opened doors to study abroad programs, especially not ones that sent girls like me to America.

And yet... There I was. Somehow, against all odds, I had made it to university. And suddenly, unbelievably, the dream I had tucked so far away I barely dared to look at it was right in front of me. I had the right to apply. I had the grades. I even had financial aid from the German government that would cover most of it.

So, I finally got my chance! I called up the study abroad office, all excited, only to be told—Oops, sorry, New York isn't possible for your schedule.

Then the lady casually said, "But Australia would work perfectly."

And what did I do? Like an absolute clown, I said:

"No, thanks. If it's not America, I'm not interested." And I hung up the phone.

I. Know.

Fast forward to a vacation with The Walking Red Flag. I was lying on the beach, miserable (as usual), stuck in yet another non-verbal cold war with him. And suddenly, it hit me: "Sisi, did you just say no to Australia? No to an escape route? Did you really just decline a way out?!"

I shot up, heart racing. I knew what I had to do. First thing I did when I got back to Munich? Called the lady back.

"Hi, yes, I've thought about it, and actually, Australia sounds great. Sign. Me. Up."

She asked me which city. Did I research? Did I compare options? Nope. I blurted out the first city I could think of—Sydney. Done. Didn't care. Just get me out of here.

I didn't tell him right away. I knew he'd try to talk me out of it, or be passive-aggressive about it, and would torture me with silence. But eventually, I broke the news. And guess what? I went.

Going to Australia was one of the bravest things I've ever done. I packed not just my suitcase, but all the courage I had left. And when I got there, I was hoping for answers, for clarity, for some kind of sign. But the first two weeks were anything but clear. I was drowning in questions. Should I stay? Should I leave? Am I being dramatic? Am I too emotional? Am I the problem? Was this just how life looks after a while—dull, heavy, full of confusion and self-doubt?

And then... came the moment.

I was in Melbourne, lying in a quiet hotel room. The morning sun was soft, golden, and kind. It crept through the window in that slow, quiet way that makes you feel like the world is holding its breath just for you. The air was warm. Still. Peaceful.

And in that gentle silence, something inside me stirred. A voice.

It whispered, Maybe this is just life now, Sisi. Maybe happiness isn't for you anymore. Maybe that ease, that lightness of be-ing—that's only for the young, the naive, the ones who haven't seen too much. Maybe this is just what growing up looks like. You settle. You accept. You stop dreaming. You learn to live without joy. I mean, I have seen many examples like that throughout my life.

And for a terrifying moment, I believed it. I thought about my aunt, years ago in Morocco, telling me in the car, "This is life. You just settle." In that hotel room, it came crashing back like a prophecy I never wanted to fulfill.

Maybe she was right, I thought.

But then, something else rose up. Fiercer. Louder. A deeper truth. A voice I hadn't heard in a long time. My own.

No, it said. Absolutely not.

If there was even a 1% chance that I could be happy again... even if I had to break up, even if I never found love again, even if I ended up alone for the rest of my life... that sliver of hope was worth more than a 100% guarantee of misery. I would rather be alone and free than attached to something that was slowly killing my spirit.

So right there, wrapped in that golden sunlight and hard-earned clarity, I chose myself.

And I want you, reading this right now, to really let that sink in. Because this—this right here—is what they call the hero's journey. This was the moment my entire life began to shift. In that quiet, ordinary hotel room, I made an extraordinary decision: I bet on me. I made the kind of decision that felt impossible, that I had avoided for so many years, four years to be exact. But something in my bones, in my roots, in the deepest part of me finally said: You deserve more. Even after years of being made to feel small, or too much, or not enough, I believed, truly believed, that I deserved happiness. I didn't need anyone else to validate that. I knew. And I trusted myself. And I really believe I was rewarded for that.

Because from that moment on... everything began to change.

I picked up my phone—old school style—and I typed a simple message.

It's over. Or something like that.

No dramatic speech. No trying to explain what he would only twist anyway. No more gaslighting. No more manipulation. Just a full stop.

I hit send.

And in that exact second, I felt something shift.

I felt free.

It didn't erase all the bad memories. It didn't undo the years.

But it gave me back me.

And for the first time in a long time, I remembered what that felt like.

From that moment on, my Australian experience was magic. I traveled, met incredible people, ate kangaroo (sorry, Australia), learned how to surf, skateboard, and even do a handstand. I rediscovered myself. I lost the weight (both the bodyweight and the fiance's toxic narcissist weight), I felt alive. I built friendships that lasted years.

And then, when my study abroad ended, I thought—Why stop now?

So, I packed my bags and went backpacking through Indonesia and Thailand. People warned me, "Be careful traveling alone as a girl!" But let me tell you—it was amazing. I met new friends, lived fully, and proved to myself that I was strong, capable, and whole—on my own.

And just when I thought life couldn't get any better, I met up with my sister in Thailand. And what happened next changed my entire life.

But that? That's for the next chapter.

THE LESSON & REFLECT RITUAL

The Lesson

Sometimes we stay in places that hurt us, not because we don't want more,

but because we're scared we won't survive without what's familiar.

But safety isn't the same as peace.

Comfort isn't the same as joy.

And staying small to keep someone else comfortable?

That's not love. That's self-abandonment.

You are not too old. You are not too late.

You are not hard to love, and your dreams are not ridiculous.

You just forgot how powerful you are when you choose you.

The moment you decide that even a sliver of joy is worth more than a guaranteed life of numbness—

That's the moment the door swings wide open.

And that's when everything begins to change.

Let's get practical.

It's time to reflect and rise.

REFLECT RITUAL – CHAPTER 13: The Moment I Gambled on Myself and Won

"Even If It's Just 1%, I'll Choose Me Every Time"

Your Tools:

• A quiet space

• A mirror

• Your phone (open voice memo or camera)

• 3 minutes of courage

Your Reflect Ritual (Say these out loud):

1. "One place in my life I stayed too long was…"

(It might be a relationship, a job, a friendship, or a version of yourself. Name it with love, not shame.)

2. "I stayed because I believed…"

(Dig into the belief that held you there. Was it fear? Guilt? Feeling like you didn't deserve more?)

3. "But now I know that my freedom looks like…"

(Speak it clearly. Describe what joy, peace, self-trust, or self-love feels like to you.)

4. "A time I chose myself, even when it was hard, was…"

(Remind yourself of a moment where you stood tall, even shaking. Celebrate it.)

5. "I rise because…"

(Wrap it in power. In truth. In knowing that choosing yourself is never the wrong move.)

Optional:

Write this in your book:

"This chapter reminded me that I am allowed to walk away from anything that asks me to shrink."

Need support?

Scan the QR code to hear me guide you through this Reflect Ritual.

Because when you bet on yourself,
you never walk away empty—you walk away free.

The best thing I have ever worn was his love.

— Sisi Surgant

CHAPTER FOURTEEN

THE LOVE STORY THAT WAS MEANT TO BE

This chapter is for my John, the love of my life, my biggest love, my everything, my one and only. The man who, in one single moment, changed the entire course of my life.

So, as I said in the last chapter, what happened in Thailand changed everything.

Picture this: I'm walking through the paradise island of Koh Phi Phi, the kind of place that looks like it was stolen straight from The Beach movie.... Fun fact: It actually was filmed on that island. No cars, just winding little streets, palm trees swaying, crystal-clear water, and—let's be honest, a lot of parties.

Now, my sister and I weren't exactly on a joy stroll. She had a pretty nasty cut from the night before (let's not get into that story), so we were on a mission, find the pharmacy/clinic where she got her stitches for a follow-up appointment. We just couldn't remember where it was since we didn't get the address.

And while I was mid-conversation, casually talking about some other guy I had met (yes, some other guy, can you believe it?), my eyes suddenly locked onto him. The man of a man. Sitting in front of a bar like a Greek god (funny because he actually is partially Greek) on vacation, trying to make a little extra cash for further backpacking by selling boat tickets to tourists.

I immediately turned to my sister and said, "Forget the guy I was just talking about. Did you see that man?! Let's go talk to him."

I didn't even hesitate. I told my sister, "Ask him where the pharmacy is. He looks like he knows his way around."

So we walked up to him. I played it super cool, of course, like I don't even see him. He had this mysterious, slightly too cool energy. At first, I thought he was being a little arrogant (spoiler alert: he was just shy). But then, I noticed something.

He was doing weird movements with his hands. I leaned in, trying to figure it out. Is he... rolling a joint? No. The man was peeling an egg. An. Egg. I looked at him. He looked at me. His face turned red. He panicked, shoved the entire egg into his mouth, and mumbled through a full mouth, "I'm hungry."

And that was the moment I knew this man was the cutest thing I had ever seen.

But did I stay? Nope.

I thought he wasn't interested, so we left. Moved on with our night. Had an amazing time. And every time I spotted him that evening on party island, I did what any mature, self-assured adult would do: I ducked, dodged, and disappeared. Because the last thing I wanted was for him to see me with this other guy.

Little did I know, he'd been looking for me all night.

Life really has a sense of humor. Like the dramatic kind.

Fast forward to the next morning. Thailand heat? Unforgiving. Sun? Way too bright. Me? Hungover, dehydrated, and reevaluating all my life choices, especially the ones involving cocktails with tiny umbrellas. I know, shocking—I rarely drink. But hey, Thailand happened. And if my parents ever read this... just skip this chapter, please.

I was sitting on the curb in front of a tiny pharmacy, waiting for my sister to grab some electrolytes or something that could bring me back to life. Hair? A situation. Skin? Glowing, but like, in an overheated way. Outfit? Let's just say I was dressed for survival, not seduction. I was doing my best to hide behind my hands and pretend I was invisible.

And then, of course, he appeared.

There he was, walking by like some gym ad or like someone poured water on him. Fresh from a workout, glistening, all muscles and sweat and that "I lift weights... and probably women too" kind of vibe. Like, sir. It's too early for this level of attraction. Calm down.

He waved.

And I thought, "Phew, okay. He's walking by. He didn't really see me. Good."

But then? He stopped.

Turned around.

Walked back.

And sat.

Right next to me. On the curb.

Like it was the most natural thing in the world.

And I swear, I panicked for a second, because what was my face even doing? Was I sitting like a normal person or melting into the concrete? But he just looked at me and started talking like we were already friends. And somehow, it worked. He was charming, calm, and confident. No pressure. No weird vibes. Just him. And me. Sitting on a hot curb in Thailand, having a full conversation like we weren't both glistening (him attractively, me... hmmm).

We exchanged Facebook, because that's just what you do when you're backpacking. You don't use your phone plan, it's way too expensive. But Facebook? That was gold. You just find a hostel or café with Wi-Fi, log in, and boom, you're connected. So yeah, we became Facebook friends.

We kept chatting. And when I say chatting, I mean he called me the most beautiful girl he had ever seen in his life.

Now, I've heard those lines before. But this? Somehow, I believed him. And just like that, our little Thai island romance turned into something much bigger.

He quit his little island job. And chased me to another dream island Ko Tao.

I remember feeling a mix of excitement and sheer panic. Like, was he really as cute as I remembered? Or had my sun-soaked, cocktail-fueled brain played tricks on me?

Then, he arrived in Koh Tao. I spotted him walking toward me in the dark, and—Oh. My. God.

This man. This. Man.

An Adonis. A real-life, stop-you-in-your-tracks, not-even-Hollywood-could-compare kind of man. Brad Pitt? Jason Momoa? The Rock? Not even close. He was it.

And I was so nervous—something that never happens—that the first words out of my mouth were: "Welcome to your honeymoon."

(Side note: Extra funny because, plot twist, I was sharing a hotel room with a complete stranger. Mom and Dad, if you are still reading, please stop.)

That night, we had the most ridiculously romantic first date. A beach. A fire show. The kind of magic you don't even believe happens in real life. The deepest conversations.

And then... we did something crazy.

We spent a full week traveling through Thailand, on tuk-tuks, boats, and yes, a freaking motorcycle. Just me, him, and sometimes my sister, who, by the way, was a blessing. She was with us almost the whole time, third-wheeling like a champ, but not in a weird way. Honestly, I've never seen her so calm, so at peace. Thailand did something good for her soul. She was glowing, relaxed, soaking up life like a warm breeze. It was beautiful to see.

But back to the romance.

There I was, holding onto a man I barely knew—who would one day become my husband—not knowing that yet, of course. Just me, him, the wind, the open road, and the sound of the ocean never too far away. Hair wild. Skin sun-kissed. Heart wide open. Riding through the hills and palm trees of Ko Tao on a motorcycle like we were in some indie movie. Paradise doesn't even begin to cover it.

And in those moments... I felt something I hadn't felt in years. Maybe ever.

Pure, raw, unfiltered happiness.

Not the kind you post about. The kind you feel in your bones. The kind where you take a deep breath and think, Oh. This. This is what life is supposed to feel like.

I had never felt so free.

But then we had to say goodbye.

We hugged at the hostel. One of those long, silent, "please freeze time" kind of hugs. And then my sister and I headed to the airport, back to beautiful Germany. Back to reality.

When we landed after that exhausting long-haul flight, I remember sitting in my childhood home, everything familiar—but I felt like I had just left a dream I wasn't ready to wake up from. Was this it? Would I ever hear from him again? Or was it one of those travel romances that burn bright and then just... fade?

I had no clue.

I took a nap. My sister and I went downstairs to grab some ice cream with a friend. We were sitting there, licking cones and pretending life was back to normal—and then my phone rang.

It was him.

My stomach flipped. Butterflies. Full-on fireworks. I couldn't believe he was actually calling me. Somehow, I had half-convinced myself that the fairytale ended when we said goodbye.

But it didn't.

He called. We talked. And from that moment on, we never stopped. Every single day, we called or messaged each other. We got to know each other deeper than I thought was even possible through a screen. We missed each other like crazy. But neither of us knew what this was—was it love? Just a crush? Were we even dating?

What I did know was: I couldn't stop thinking about him. And clearly, he couldn't stop thinking about me.

One night, on yet another marathon phone call, we admitted it—we didn't want it to end. So we made a plan.

We were going to meet again. In Vietnam.

He had always dreamed of seeing Vietnam. And I had caught the travel bug so badly I would've followed adventure anywhere—especially if it meant seeing him again. But there was a catch: money. I was broke, having just returned from months of travel.

So I hustled.

I picked up a waitress job even though I'm honestly not a good waitress. But it was fast cash. I worked every single day, skipping time with friends, just to save every euro. I even spent part of it getting my nails, hair, and brows done—I mean, come on, I had to show up looking like a goddess, right?

My mom thought I was crazy. She said, "You're really flying across the world again—for a boy?" I told her, "I just know. I trust myself. I have to see him."

And on his side? Same chaos. His family didn't get it either. "Why are you flying to Vietnam for a girl?" And he simply said, "Because I promised her."

And so we did it.

We both booked our flights. The day before I left, I was so nervous and excited I couldn't sleep. Then I packed my bag, boarded that flight, and landed in Vietnam—heart pounding. He had arrived earlier and was waiting for me at the airport.

I'll never forget that moment.

I saw him standing there and my whole body melted. Butterflies? Try a full-blown migration. I ran into his arms and we hugged like we were finally home. Then we grabbed a taxi, figured out a hostel, and jumped into the next chapter of our story.

We were going to backpack the whole country—top to bottom, left to right—the full adventure. And we did. Nearly a whole month, just the two of us, dragging backpacks and dreams across rice fields, mountains, beaches, restaurants, scooters, and a whole lot of long, questionable bus rides.

Let me be clear:

Traveling as a couple?

The ultimate relationship test.

You see each other at your best, your worst, your hangriest, and your "Whose idea was this hostel?" breaking point. You fight over silly things. You get lost. You lose your bags and find them again. You nearly break up over weird humor.

But we passed. With flying colors.

It was chaotic and magical and intimate in a way only backpacking can be.

It felt sexy.

It felt like: this is it. This is real.

And okay, now that I think about it, this part makes me laugh to this day.

Because while we were traveling through Vietnam, we made up a story that we were on our honeymoon. Like, freshly married. We told everyone. Seriously—restaurants, tour guides, random hotel staff, random people.

And the best part? People believed us.

We got free desserts, special seats, sweet little notes—like it was official. We thought we were hilarious.

But looking back now... maybe we manifested it.

Because, spoiler alert: We actually got married a year and a half later.

Yup. For real. We still laugh about it sometimes, like—"Damn, we really called it, huh?"

And what nobody knew—not even him—was that deep inside, secretly, quietly...

That was my biggest wish.

That story we made up?

That was my dream come true.

So naturally...

I had to break up with him again...

In my head.

Because that's what we do, right?

The happier we feel, the louder the voice in our head says, "This is too good. This can't be real. Shut it down, Sisi. Shut it down before it breaks your heart."

And then came the voice of logic.

He lives in America.

You live in Germany.

You love your family.

You are your family.

You're not moving across the world for a guy.

Be logical. Be mature. Be German.

But the universe? Oh, she had plans.

He came to visit me in Germany.

Met my mom. Met my friends.

And everyone loved him.

Worse—he loved them too.

I was completely, absolutely, undeniably trapped in love.

But still, I fought it. Told myself, "Nope. This can't work. Too far. Too different. Too young. Too scary."

So we tried to move on.

And I hate to admit it, but yeah... we went on dates with other people.

(Sorry, kids, if you're reading this—we had a little side quest.)

But some connections? You just can't walk away from.

He was always in my head. Always the standard. Always the "ugh, this guy isn't even close to him" comparison. And always on my phone line.

And then one day,

He called me.

And in his calm, sweet voice, he said, "Do you want to go on a Valentine's date with me?"

I assumed he meant a cute little Zoom date. You know, a virtual dinner, maybe a playlist. No. He meant he had just bought me a plane ticket to America.. My jaw? On the floor. My heart? On a roller coaster.

And here's the thing: I knew his parents and family were totally against us. On paper, we were chaos. I was older. I was Arabic. I came from a different culture, and I lived halfway across the world.

Not exactly the dream daughter-in-law his family envisioned. And my own family? Equally unimpressed. They wanted me to be practical—build a career in Germany, use my degrees, which I had worked so hard for, and stay close.

But love?

Love doesn't do practical.

So I said yes.

And when I landed, he gave me the most unforgettable week of my life. He wined me, dined me, showed me off, and made me feel like I was the only woman in the world. It was surreal. He was everything—thoughtful, confident, tender, bold. The kind of man you think only exists in books or dreams.

I'd dated Germans before—sweet, respectful, low-drama. I loved the freedom in those relationships. But I often missed the heat. The fire. The take-the-lead energy. Then he came along: an American with the heart of a Mediterranean man. Strong, romantic, a protector—but without the need to control. The perfect mix I didn't even know I was searching for. I looked at him and thought: Oh no. I'm in real trouble.

Because I was falling. Deep.

I went back to Germany dazed and lovesick. But the connection wouldn't fade. So we made a plan: After I finished my semester in

July, I'd come for ninety days on an visa waiver program, just to see. To live together, to figure things out, to know if this was truly it. No pressure. No promises. Just love and possibility.

Those three months? Heaven. Not perfect, but real. We laughed, fought, made up, danced in the kitchen, and cried on the couch. We knew how to fight. We knew how to love. I had never experienced something so safe and electric at the same time.

I flew back home, aching, counting the days until I could return. One month later, I came back for his birthday, for Christmas, for love. But then the nightmare hit.

At immigration, they pulled me into secondary inspection. Asked me question after question. Searched my bags. Opened my Facebook messages. Treated me like a criminal, oras if I had something to hide.

Are you working illegally? Are you trying to stay in the U.S.?

No. I was just in love.

But they didn't care. They told me I had stayed too long before. I could only stay six more weeks—and after that, I was banned from entering the U.S. for a whole year.

A whole year.

I was devastated. We both were. This wasn't a casual romance anymore—this was it. And suddenly, the love of my life was being ripped away by a stamp in a passport. We sat together in silence, holding hands, hearts breaking. The future felt blurry. He couldn't leave his new job. I wasn't allowed to come back. It felt impossible.

But real love doesn't fold.

It was winter. The world wrapped in snow, hushed and glowing. Christmas lights shimmered above us like a sky full of tiny stars. He took me on a horse-drawn carriage ride—just the two of us, tucked beneath wool blankets, our fingers intertwined, breath rising in clouds.

And then—I saw it.
A blinking sign, bold and unmistakable:
Will you marry me?

He didn't ask with words.
He just knew.

He wasn't going to let me go. Not to a different country, not to a different life. He got down on one knee, heart first, full of fire.

And for the first time in my life, I didn't hesitate.

No fear. No doubt. Just truth.

It was the easiest yes I've ever said.

This time, it was real.

I said yes. And I stayed.

And now we go back and forth for vacation and to visit my family in Germany, Morocco, and Tunisia, and they come to visit us all the time. What a blessing and adventure, especially for our kids. Giving them the gift of traveling and exploring different cultures is just the best gift we can give them. I am happy I can pass on to my kids what I got from my parents. Everything turned out so beautifully.

We began to build our life in St. Louis, Missouri, and we made everything work—long-distance, green card process (believe me that wasn't easy or cheap), visas, family approvals, every hurdle in the book.

And now? Everyone loves everyone. My family adores him. His family adores me (at least that's what I tell myself, lol). We have built a beautiful, crazy, once-in-a-lifetime love story and life.

And I wouldn't change a single thing.

Sometimes, I still can't believe my luck—how I ended up here, in this life that feels like a dream. The dream man. The dream kids. The dream love. I catch myself in quiet moments—at the dinner table, during bedtime snuggles, or even just folding tiny socks—and I look around thinking, Is this really mine?

I still can't believe I got my happy ending.

And when I think about my husband—this man with the kindest heart, the strongest integrity, the way he leads with love and stands with humility, and the way he treats my family and loves them. He takes care of everyone and everything; it all makes sense. Of course, he turned out this amazing. Just look at where he comes from. I truly hit the jackpot not just with him, but with his whole family.

His parents are the kind of people who teach you life's biggest lessons just by being themselves.

My mother-in-law is steady, faithful, and quietly wise. She never needed big speeches—her kindness, strength, and grounded presence said it all. When I moved here, she was the first to make space for me. She took me to lunch, listened, showed up. She made me feel like I belonged. Honestly, she became my first best friend here—and still is. I don't know what bonded us—maybe our shared values, maybe our quiet strength. Maybe it's that neither of us can ever say no to ice cream. Whatever it is, I'm so grateful.

My father-in-law has a heart of gold. He's the first to show up—and you will get his help, whether you ask for it or not. He's the kind of man who makes you feel safe, just by being in the room.

And then there's my sister-in-law. I didn't just gain family—I gained a sister. She's the one I call when something's funny or something's hard. Her husband is like a real brother to me. And their kids? I love them like my own.

Even my brother-in-law's parents love my kids like grandparents would—because that's what they've become. A third set. A bonus we never expected.

I never imagined loving my in-laws this much. But I do. They're not just his people anymore. They're mine. And somehow, against all odds, I got my happy ending.

Remember how my aunt once told me in Morocco that a girl will never marry the love of her life—the one great, all-consuming love? That kind of love, she believed, wasn't real. But I guess I proved her wrong. And I know that she is so happy and proud of me because she keeps telling me that she is so grateful, because I did find real love. The kind of love that doesn't waver. The kind that stands the test of time, distance, and every hurdle life throws in its way.

Because love—true love—conquers all. The miles, the burdens, the doubts, the fears. It silences the voices that say it's impossible. It defies the odds. I have him, and he has me. Forever. And that, after everything, is my happy ending.

THE LESSON & REFLECT RITUAL

The Lesson

Real love doesn't ask you to shrink.

It doesn't control, confuse, or make you doubt your worth.

It doesn't need chasing, convincing, or pretending.

Real love feels like home.

It's not perfect—but it's safe.

It's honest, it's deep, and it shows up—over and over again.

Sometimes, you have to walk away from what you thought was love

to make space for the kind that actually is.

The kind that sees you. Holds you. Stays.

And when it comes... let it.

Let it hold you. Let it melt the walls. Let it prove you wrong in the best way.

Because no matter what they told you...

You are not too much. You are not too loud. You are not too old. You are not too late.

You are worthy of the kind of love that makes you believe in fairy tales again.

Even if your happy ending looks nothing like the story you imagined, it's yours. And it's beautiful. Probably even better than you imagined.

Let's get practical.

It's time to reflect and rise.

REFLECT RITUAL – CHAPTER 14: The Love Story That Was Meant to Be

"I Am Worthy of the Kind of Love That Stays"

Your Tools:

• A quiet space

• A mirror

• Your phone (open voice memo or camera)

• 3 minutes of courage

Your Reflect Ritual (Say these out loud):

1. "A love I once thought was everything, but wasn't, was..."

(Be honest. Say the name, the feeling, the story you carried.)

2. "What that love taught me about myself was..."

(Did it wake you up? Did it break you down? Did it help you realize what you'll never accept again?)

3. "Now I know that real love looks like..."

(Paint it clearly. Is it safe? Passionate? Playful? Grounded? Speak it into your life.)

4. "One way I've chosen love over fear is..."

(Think of a time you risked being seen. When you stayed open, even after being hurt.)

5. "I rise because..."

(Because you are love. Because you choose love. Because you are finally ready to receive it, fully.)

Optional:

Write this in your book:

"This chapter reminded me that I am worthy of the kind of love that makes me feel seen, safe, and completely myself."

Need support?

Scan the QR code to hear me guide
you through this Reflect Ritual.

Because the right love doesn't take
away from you, it builds with you.

The real strength of a woman is revealed in the way she carries herself.

— Sisi Surgant

Chapter Fifteen

THE LONELIEST LOVE STORY THAT TURNED INTO HOME

So, there I was. Moved to America.

More specifically? Not even St. Louis, but St. Charles, Missouri. If you're imagining me sipping espresso at a little European-style café, people-watching, casually strolling downtown like I did in Germany: *Think again!*

Because the first time I tried that? I got dressed all cute, thought, Ooh, let's have a little European moment! And drove more than half an hour to downtown St. Louis, ready to live my best city life.

And what did I find? Practically a ghost town.

I mean, where was everyone? Back home, city centers are alive, full of people, cafés buzzing, energy in the air. Here? It felt empty. Unlike European cities, where the downtown is a cultural and social hub, St. Louis is different. People don't flock to the city center for casual strolls or spontaneous coffee dates. The energy is scattered, spread out into different pockets—suburbs, strip malls, cozy little neighborhoods you'd never find unless you knew where to look. And St. Charles? Even more suburban. Think historic charm, but on a much smaller scale, where life moves at a slower, quieter pace.

Let's just say my European reality didn't exactly translate.

And then? Reality smacked me in the face. The reality of moving for love. John had to go back to work (because, duh, we need to eat), and I was stuck at home.

No job (thanks to my green card process).

No way to travel (thanks to my green card process).

No friends (thanks to moving to a place where I knew absolutely no one).

Just me, alone, in a new country, staring at the walls, contemplating all my life choices. And loneliness hits differently when you're in love. I was the happiest I had ever been with John. But at the same time, I had never felt so alone in my life.

I cried a lot. I FaceTimed my parents and siblings every day, sobbing, trying to bridge the impossible distance between us through a screen. One day, during our call, my dad sighed and said, "Sisi, you will always be a stranger in that country. Come back home."

Oof. Right in the gut.

There I was, fighting so hard for the love of my life, finally happy in love... and yet, it felt like I had to sacrifice everything else.
My family.
My friends.
My culture.
My entire life.

And it hurt. Why can't life ever be easy?

I kept asking myself: Why do we always have to choose?
Why can't we just have it all?
Why couldn't I be with John and still keep my family close?
Why couldn't I build a life in a new country without having to let go of the old one?

It felt like the most emotionally overwhelming experience I had ever gone through.

I used to daydream about teleportation—how amazing it would be to spend my days in Munich, laughing with my family and friends, then zip back to the U.S. in the evening to be with John. I missed them so much. Especially my sister—my ride-or-die, my best friend in the whole world. My parents and the feeling of a security net. My brother and his silly humor, he is my rock. My lovely nephew, who means the world to me, I was very involved in his life, like his second mom basically.

And of course, my mind spiraled. I started catastrophizing. What if something happened to my dad, with his health issues? What if something happened to my mom?

And I couldn't even get on a plane if I needed to. The stupid green card process had me stuck, unable to travel, unable to move, feeling completely powerless.

I'm telling you, this kind of loneliness was unlike anything I'd ever experienced.
It hit me in a way I never saw coming.

Somewhere in the middle of all the chaos, we got married.

For legal reasons (green card things, you know how it goes), John and I had a small courthouse wedding first. No big party. No fancy dress (but I still looked cute—like really cute). Just us and our closest family. I officially became Mrs. Surgant.

But here's the thing no one tells you: even after saying "I do," even after legally being married to the love of your life, the loneliness didn't just disappear. Because as much as I loved John, I needed my own life, too.

I've always been independent. I never wanted to be that person who only has their partner and nobody else (nothing wrong with that, but I needed my own thing!). I'm a very social person. A total social butterfly.

I need community, connection, my own thing outside of "wife."

And one day, my sister, the genius, hit me with:

Her: "Why don't you just go on Bumble BFF?"

Me: "Excuse me?! I am married."

Her: "Not the dating part, Sisi. The BFF part. It's for making friends!"

Me: "BFF mode? To find friends? In America? Who does that? No offense, but who does that?!"

I thought it would just be weirdos. But desperate times, my friends. Desperate times.

So, I downloaded the app, and to my absolute surprise, I found amazing people. My little lifeline in St. Louis.

That's when things started to shift. Making friends, finding my own rhythm, figuring out how to actually live here—that's when things started feeling better.More real. More grounded.

And then September happened.

The wedding of our dreams.

My family flew in. Both of our families were there. Friends from all over came. The love in the air was electric—you could feel it. And having my family with me, physically by my side in this new world I now call home, meant everything.

But there's one part that still makes my heart burst: my amazing nephew came. He probably doesn't even know how much that meant to me. I'm still so happy, so grateful, so moved that he was there. He even brought his best friend with him, who I've basically adopted in my heart as a second nephew. Having those two incredible young men at our wedding, standing with us, celebrating us... It touched me more deeply than I can put into words. And my nephew? He wasn't just a guest—he stood in the wedding, right there with my husband. That moment... that was joy.

Still, my heart ached a little. My brother, my other best friend, couldn't make it. And that was hard. He's my protector, my day-one, the one who would move mountains for me. He, my sister, and I we're the forever trio. Loud, loving, unbreakable. We fight hard, love harder, and the world better not come for one of us, because the other two will rise like fire. We fight in private, but protect in public—ride or die, always. And even though he couldn't be there in person, he was there in my heart every single second.

We had it all. A Moroccan wedding. An American wedding. A Moroccan-Tunisian henna night. It wasn't just a celebration—it was an explosion of cultures, traditions, and joy that made it feel like we were stepping into our very own fairytale.

Our celebrations began on Friday night with a heartfelt rehearsal dinner—a beautiful blend of cultures meeting over laughter, and the buzz of excitement in the air. It was the calm before the storm, the soft opening to the most unforgettable weekend of our lives.

Then came Saturday: the henna night, a cherished tradition held the evening before a wedding.

Surrounded by family and friends, music, and the sweet smell of Arabic pastries and mint tea, we gathered in celebration. I wore a deep red velvet kaftan, rich and royal, as is tradition for the bride, either red or green to honor blessing, protection, and love. My hands were adorned with delicate, intricate henna designs, each swirl a symbol of joy and luck. John wore a traditional white Moroccan men's kaftan, a long, robe-like garment with classic embroidery down the front—elegant, simple, and full of heritage.

His hands were also marked with henna—just a touch, a shared symbol between us. My girlfriends and guests joined in, excitedly comparing their designs as they ate and laughed.

And the food? My mama cooked it all. A massive pot of traditional couscous with chicken, steaming and fragrant, made with love and generations of history. The table overflowed with homemade pastries, honey-soaked sweets, and mint tea in sparkling glasses—it was the taste of home, served with pride and joy.

And then came the big day.

I walked down the aisle on my father's arm, and it was one of the most emotional moments of my life. My dad, proud and steady, holding onto me like the little girl he once carried, now walking me into my future. I wore a timeless white dress, classic and elegant, just like the little girl in me had always dreamed. But the night didn't end there. Later, I transformed into a traditional queen, draped in a Moroccan kaftan—a breathtaking white, floor-length gown covered in intricate golden embroidery, paired with traditional gold jewelry that shimmered with every step. It was regal. It was tradition. It was me.

John—my Arabic king—made jaws drop when he changed into a traditional Moroccan jabador, a silky tunic and matching trousers, topped with a majestic selham, the flowing cape that drapes over the shoulders like royalty. And let me tell you... He looked so good, basically like a real-life Aladdin, minus the flying carpet.

The celebration was in full swing when our belly dancer entered. Draped in silk and gold coins, she danced her way into the room like a flame—hips swaying, veil floating, captivating every soul in the room. The music, the movement, the energy—she brought the rhythm of North Africa alive, and the entire room came alive with her.

Then it was time for the grand moment—the amarias.

In traditional Moroccan weddings, the bride and groom are carried on intricately decorated platforms or chairs, high above the crowd like royalty. And yes—we did that too. Except, we had to get creative. You can't exactly find amarias on Amazon or in a St. Louis specialty shop. So we built them. With love, sweat, and the help of a talented friend, we crafted our own Moroccan-style amarias—platforms draped in fabric, lined with cushions, held up by poles—and then, with the strength of John's football friends (because my man is 270 pounds!), we were carried through the crowd, lifted like a king and queen, with cheers and howls echoing through the room.

And the magic didn't stop there. Guests were treated to a delicious spread of Asian food, a tribute to the place we met—Thailand. It was our way of honoring the beginning of our love story, weaving it into this moment of forever.

Arabic music pulsed through the speakers—Darija beats mixed with Tunisian rhythms—and the energy was pulsating. We danced until our feet hurt and our cheeks ached from smiling. There was so much laughter, so much music, and so much love—it poured out of every corner of the room.

It was, without a doubt, the best day of our lives.

And finally, for the first time since I moved here, I felt it—I was home.

That was the moment I realized—home isn't just a place. It's what you build. Yes, I missed my family. Yes, it was (and still is) hard.

But suddenly, it wasn't so bad. Slowly... it stopped feeling impossible. It didn't hurt quite as much. We have WhatsApp, and I FaceTime my family every day. We have planes. Germany isn't gone, it's a plane ride away.

And guess what? My family started visiting us all the time, too. Especially my sister.

Being apart from her? It was (and still is) one of the hardest parts of this whole journey.

I honestly thought I'd never get over the homesickness.

But I always have to go through that pain. Even now, every time we say goodbye—whether I'm leaving them or they're leaving me—it stings. That ache doesn't go away. But I've learned how to carry it. You learn to manage it and appreciate what you have in front of you. I've learned how to balance the longing with gratitude. Because, as hard as it is, we do see each other way more than I ever expected.

And I've realized...

The world wasn't as big as I thought.

Love really does make everything possible. Cheesy but true.

THE LESSON & REFLECT RITUAL

The Lesson

Love can move you across the world, but it takes courage, grit, and a whole lot of self-work to truly feel at home.

Moving for love sounds romantic—and it *is*—but the truth is, even the deepest love doesn't erase homesickness, identity loss, or loneliness. You can be head over heels and still feel completely out of place. You can be building a life with your soulmate and still cry because you miss your sister or your mom's couscous. That doesn't make you weak. That makes you *human*.

I had to learn that home isn't where you're from—it's what you create. And that doesn't happen overnight. It happens in the little things: learning the rhythm of a new city, finding your people (even if it means swiping right on Bumble BFF), and making room for both where you came from and where you're going.

You don't have to choose between love and your roots. You just have to be brave enough to carry both.

And girl, if I can build a life, a community, and two wedding ceremonies with a green card, a broken heart, and a kaftan—so can you.

REFLECT RITUAL – CHAPTER 15: The Loneliest Love Story That Turned Into Home

"I Can Miss What I Left—and Still Love Where I Am"

Your Tools:

• A quiet space

• A mirror

• Your phone (open voice memo or camera)

• 3 minutes of courage

Your Reflect Ritual (Say these out loud):

1. "A part of my life I had to leave behind to start something new was..."

(Say it clearly. A place, a person, a routine, a version of yourself.)

2. "What I miss most about it is..."

(Honor it. Let yourself feel the ache. The details matter.)

3. "But what I've gained by choosing this new chapter is..."

(Speak it with pride. The love. The freedom. The unexpected joys.)

4. "One way I've created a sense of home in this new life is..."

(Think of a habit, a friendship, a ritual, or a moment where it all started to feel like yours.)

5. "I rise because..."

(Because you carry love in both hands. Because you're allowed to have roots and wings.)

Optional:

Write this in your book :

"This chapter reminded me that I can hold grief in one hand and gratitude in the other, and still build something beautiful."

Need support?

Scan the QR code to hear me guide you through this Reflect Ritual.

Because building a home isn't about geography. It's about love, and the courage to keep showing up for your new beginning.

All love begins and ends there.

— Robert Browning

Chapter Sixteen

MOTHERHOOD

Ever since I was a little girl, I knew one thing for sure: I wanted to be a mom. Some kids dream of being astronauts, pop stars, or princesses. Me? Sure, I've told you how much I love to perform. But the ultimate goal? Motherhood. I didn't just want to be a mom; I felt like I was born for it.

I imagined it all. I knew I would be a rockstar mom: the one who showed up to every school event, the one who knew all the teachers by name, the one who sat at the kitchen table every night, helping with homework. I would be the kind of mom who did it better. Better than the generation before, better than anything I had seen.

Because isn't that what we all want? To take the best of what our parents gave us, mix it with everything we've learned, and create something even stronger for our own kids?

I had a plan.

And then?

Life laughed in my face.

Just when life finally felt settled—married, in love, working out, finding my rhythm—I got the big and wonderful news.

My period was always on time. And now? It wasn't.

My sister was visiting, and casually, I said,

"I think I need to take a test."

And just like that:

Pregnant.

I wanted to laugh. I wanted to cry. I wanted to scream. I wanted to do all of it at the same time. My sister and I were so thrilled. Me, finally a mom. My sister, an aunt again. We were over the moon.

John had no clue what was coming. We went out to dinner, and I secretly slipped the pregnancy test into a napkin. I set up my phone, ready to record his reaction.

"Baby, can you pass me that napkin?"

John, completely oblivious, grabbed it, felt something inside, and pulled it out.

He frowned. Turned it over in his hands.

"What is that?"

I kept my best poker face. "Yeah... what is that?"

Still clueless, he looked around and actually asked the waiter.

Holy guacamole. I nearly died of embarrassment.

Panic.

I quickly distracted the waiter and told John, "Look at it again! Read it!"

His eyes locked on the test. Widened. Froze.

"Oh. Oh! Oh! Really?"

And then, pure joy. The biggest hug, the biggest kiss, and the happiest moment of our lives.

Let me be straight with you.
Pregnancy?

Whew. Whoever says pregnancy is beautiful, are you okay?! Are you making this up?

I had preeclampsia, nausea, and swelling the size of a small country. I was miserable. Absolutely, painfully, miserable. I was not glowing. I was surviving.

At thirty-six weeks, I developed preeclampsia. My blood pressure spiked dangerously high, and the doctors made the call: I had to be induced immediately.

Induced? Induced what? What does that even mean? I had never heard that word in my life. I looked over at John, eyes wide in panic. "Wait... what do they mean? Do they really mean that? Can I run away from this situation?! Should I start running now?!"

Except, where was I supposed to run? The baby was literally inside me. There was no escaping this. No turning back. No last-minute "just kidding!" I was officially trapped in this reality. So I did the only thing I could, toughen up, breathe, and accept my fate, I guess. I was unprepared and in shock. I thought I still had four weeks to go. In my head, there was still enough time—time to prepare, time to pack my hospital bag properly—yep you read right, hospital bag not packed— time to get Instagram ready, time to process everything. But suddenly, I had no time at all.

Nothing about it felt real. I wasn't mentally prepared for the moment that would change my life forever. But there was no discussion, no room to wait. It had to happen, and it had to happen now.

And so, they induced me.

Then... we waited.

Thirty-six hours.

Thirty-six hours of labor, waiting, contractions, pain, exhaustion, waiting some more. Time stretched in the most unbearable way. It felt like it would never end. And then, just when I thought I had no strength left...

It happened.

The actual birth? A breeze. After thirty-six hours of waiting, when she was finally ready, she came out easy-peasy, like she had been waiting for the perfect moment to make her entrance.

And the second I held her... the second I felt her tiny body against mine, skin to skin, all of it—the exhaustion, the pain, the fear, the waiting—everything disappeared.

She was here.

My daughter. My Mimi. My greatest joy. And in that moment, I had everything I ever wanted.

And then, thirty minutes later, a nightmare began.

The drugs, the highs and lows of my body being pumped full of medications. I was in and out of consciousness, so exhausted I couldn't even process what was happening to me. And when I finally came back to reality? I was torn. Stitched. Bruised and broken in ways I had never been before.

But there was no time to heal.

Because there she was. My daughter. My world.

And I had one job. Be her mother. No matter how much pain I was in, no matter how much my body was screaming for rest, I had to be there. And I wanted to be. I had waited my whole life for this moment. I wasn't going to miss a second. But still, it was so intense. As mothers, the way our bodies go through trauma, and yet, within minutes, we are expected to show up as if nothing happened. As if we didn't just go through war, is unsettling.

I didn't have the luxury of "taking it easy." I didn't get to lie in bed and recover. I had to breastfeed, to wake up every two hours, to function on nothing, to love on my baby, to show up. I mean, all moms get that.

And then: baby blues. The postpartum depression, and this strange emotional rollercoaster that no one prepares you for. One minute, I was so in love I thought my heart would burst. Next, I was crying because I felt like I wasn't doing enough, even though I was doing everything.

I felt crazy. But I wasn't. I was just a new mom. Some studies say that up to twenty percent of women go through this, but we don't talk about it enough. Too many of us suffer silently, feeling like we're the only ones. But we aren't. Motherhood is beautiful, but brutal. It's love and sacrifice in the purest form.

It wasn't just the emotional shift.

It was the physical one, too.

People love to talk about pregnancy like it's some magical glow-up. They'll mention the cravings, the cute outfits, the cute bump, the "nesting." But what they don't talk about enough is what happens after. The real stuff. The stuff that hits you in the middle of the night when everyone else has gone back to their lives, and you're standing in the dark—leaking, shaking, and Googling if it's normal to cry over a wrong Thai food order.

I carried that baby for nine long, miserable months. Nausea that made me hate my favorite foods. A body that felt like it didn't belong to me anymore—swollen, like really swollen, aching, exhausted.

Then came labor. Birth. Let's just say it wasn't pretty. It was powerful, yes—but also brutal. There were stitches. There were tears. There was a version of me that shattered on that delivery table and didn't know how to come back.

And just when you think, "Okay, I survived that..."—surprise!

Now you're a mom.

No sleep. No breaks. No manual.

Your hormones are a mess, your boobs are leaking, your hair is falling out, and your soul? Honestly, it's trying to remember who she used to be.

You're food-deprived, shower-deprived, touch-deprived, yourself-deprived.

And yet—somehow—you're still expected to function. To show up. To glow.

There's this insane cocktail of love and guilt.

You look at your baby and your heart explodes... and then ten seconds later, you're wondering if you're doing enough, being enough, loving enough.

Since becoming a mom, I swear I also became an Olympic-level over-thinker.

It's like motherhood comes with this unspoken deal:

Buy one baby, get lifelong guilt and anxiety for free.

No refunds. No exchanges. But all the love in the world packed into it, too.

The sleepless nights. The exhaustion so deep it settles into the bones. The breastfeeding struggles—the hunger, the thirst, the pain. The overwhelming responsibility of it all. And caffeine? Not an option. I was so determined to breastfeed, so conscious of what went into my body, that I refused even a sip. So there I was, utterly depleted, running on nothing but pure willpower and love.

And then, one day, sitting on the edge of my bed, holding my tiny, fragile, beautiful daughter, it hit me like a train. The weight of it. The realization that I was a mom now. Not just for today, not just for this moment—for life. The old Sisi was gone.

The free-spirited girl, the one who could sleep in, the one who only had to take care of herself, the one who could leave the house without planning like a military strategist, she was gone. Just like that. Poof. She went bye-bye the moment I became a mom.

It was everything I had ever wanted. It was the best thing that had ever happened to me. And yet, there was this strange, unexpected feeling no one had prepared me for: grief. Grief for my old self. For the life I once had. For the version of me who would never exist again. We don't talk enough about that part. No one tells you that when you become a mother, you are also reborn. And like any birth, it's messy. It's painful. It requires you to leave something behind. To trust the process.

I had to learn how to love this new version of me. The one who was still me, but different. A mother. A protector. A caregiver. A woman who would never, ever come first again because my children would always come first. I had to grow into this new identity. And that's the thing about motherhood—you don't just wake up and have it all figured out. You evolve. You adjust. You stretch yourself in ways you never thought possible. And sometimes, that stretching hurts.

And just when I had started to find my footing...

Just when I thought,

"Okay. Maybe I can do this. Maybe I'm figuring it out."

Boom.

Eighteen months in... Surprise.

Pregnancy number two.

This time, John and I found out together.

And this time? A boy.

The labor with Samy was completely different. I felt ready. I labored at home, waiting until the contractions got close together. I took my time, listened to my body, and when I finally felt it was time, we headed to the hospital.

From the moment we arrived to the moment he was born? Ten hours. For some reason, I couldn't get an epidural. My veins were too small, probably dehydrated, and they just couldn't get the IV in me. And since you need an IV for an epidural... that meant I was doing this whole thing naturally.

I labored almost the entire time without medication. Finally—maybe five, ten minutes before he was born—they got the IV in and gave me the epidural.

At that point, I didn't even care about the pain relief anymore. I just wanted it because I knew I would have stitches afterward. There was no time to process anything, though, because the moment I started pushing, something primal took over.

The doctor kept telling me to take breaks. I didn't.

I pushed like a warrior, like a woman on a mission, like my body had been waiting for this moment my whole life. And then, out he came. My sunlight. All nine pounds and twelve ounces of him.

A whole linebacker. My beautiful, strong, perfect boy. But then, just when I thought I could finally exhale, the worst thing happened. He had to go to the NICU. He was full-term, big, strong. But he had trouble transitioning. He struggled to breathe. And in that moment, I felt my heart shatter into a million pieces.

And with it came something else—guilt, of course. Even though I did everything I could, even though I was with him every moment I was allowed, even though I held him, did skin-to-skin, breastfed him, and poured every ounce of love into him, I still felt like I wasn't there enough.

And even now, years later, it still haunts me.

Even though I know it wasn't my fault. Even though I know he's healthy and strong today. There's something about seeing your baby in the NICU that stays with you. And sometimes, when I look at him, I still feel that guilt creeping in.

That brutal, relentless, soul-crushing mom guilt that quietly emerges and then refuses to let go. It's maddening.

I felt it for Samy—for every hour he spent in the NICU without me, for every moment I couldn't hold him, kiss him, comfort him. But I also felt it for Mimi. My first baby. My girl who had me all to herself, who was my whole world... and now? Suddenly, she had to share it all. Share her mama. Share her dad. Share her space. And it broke me.

And just when I thought I had the balance figured out, the guilt flipped. I'd be giving Mimi my time, and suddenly I'd feel like I was abandoning Samy. Then I'd be with Samy, and guilt would whisper, But what about Mimi?

It was constant. No matter what I did, I felt like I was failing someone.

And I started wondering... Who even am I now? Where did that carefree, light-hearted Sisi go? The one who used to move through life with ease?

She felt so far away.

And that's when I finally understood. Yes, I had lost a part of myself. Yes, I would never be the old Sisi again. But in that loss, I became something greater.

I became a mother.

I became a warrior.

And my greatest gifts?

Mimi and Samy.

My heart. My soul. My biggest joy. My ultimate flex.

I always pictured raising my kids in Germany. In my language, in my culture. The same parks I played in. The same school system I grew up in—only this time, I'd understand how it works. I'd know how to show up for my kids in all the ways I once needed. I imagined familiarity and family—my children running through Oma's house, my sister nearby, my brother dropping in for tea. My village, my roots, my people.

Instead? I found myself a mother in America.

New country. New system. No family nearby. And absolutely no clue what I was doing.

And while I say all this, while I pour out my heart for my babies, I need to give a huge shoutout to my husband, my rock, my partner for life, my John. Because I am nothing without him. We are a team. He is just as much my absolute everything. I could not breathe easy without him. Through every high, every low, every struggle, every triumph, he has been there, holding me up, walking beside me, and being the best dad ever. I am so blessed to have him, so grateful for his love.

And as I sit here now, a few years later, watching them both grow—Mimi with her bold heart and gentle wisdom, Samy with his strong spirit and sunshine smile—I am in complete awe of what my body, my heart, and my soul have carried. I love that they are best friends.

Motherhood cracked me open in places I didn't know existed.

It rearranged my insides.

It challenged everything I thought I knew about myself.

It wrecked me and rebuilt me, again and again.

It taught me to surrender.

To let go of the idea of being perfect.

To redefine strength, not as having it all together, but as showing up, even when I felt like I had nothing left to give.

I've cried on the floor.

I've rocked babies with sore arms and puffy eyes.

I've whispered, You've got this, Sisi, through gritted teeth and tired lips.

I've smiled through pain.

Laughed through chaos.

And loved harder than I ever thought humanly possible.

And the wildest part?

I'd do it all again. Every second. Every stitch. Every tear. Every moment of messy, glorious, aching love.

Because this—*this*—is the greatest role of my life.

Not the brands. Not the shows. Not the stage.

But *this*.

Being their mama.

And I know—one day, they'll grow up.

They'll find their own wings. Their own people. Their own path.

But I'll always be here.

Cheering them on.

Loving them louder than life.

Praying over them loud and in silence.

Holding their stories in my chest.

Because once you become a mother, you are never not one again.

Even when one day they no longer fit in your arms, they'll live forever in your soul.

And if you're a mama reading this?

Let me just say this:

You're not alone.

In the exhaustion.

In the guilt.

In the joy.

In the heartbreak.

In the love so big it swallows you whole.

You're not alone.

You're seen.

You're sacred.

You're strong.

And this wild, beautiful, brutal, breathtaking thing called motherhood?

You're doing it.

And you're doing it beautifully.

THE LESSON & REFLECT RITUAL

The Lesson

You weren't born knowing how to mother.

You became one—through blood, tears, stitches, sleepless nights, and fierce, immeasurable love.

You thought motherhood would be soft.

But it broke you open—and you rebuilt stronger.

You thought you had to choose—between your old self and this new one.

But your heart expanded, and now you carry both.

You didn't lose yourself.

You found the version of you who shows up—tired but present, overwhelmed but willing.

Not perfect, but powerful.

You are not behind.

You are not failing.

You are a living, breathing, soft-spoken warrior.

You are exactly who you were meant to be. Your past self still exists, but now she is connected together with the version of you today, stronger, wiser, unstoppable. That combination? That's your superpower.

You don't need to have it all together to be everything your children need.

Your presence is your power.

And the love you give? It multiplies.

Let's reflect.

You've earned this moment.

REFLECT RITUAL – CHAPTER 16: Motherhood

"I Don't Glow—I Grow."

Your Tools:

• A quiet space

• A mirror

• Your phone (open voice memo or camera)

• 3 minutes of courage

Your Reflect Ritual (Say these out loud):

1. "One expectation I had about motherhood that didn't

match reality was..."

(Was it the way you thought you'd feel after birth? The way you thought love would feel? The way your body or emotions would bounce back?)

2. "One part of me I feared losing in motherhood was..."

(The carefree version? The ambitious one? The woman who had time to dream and dance, and shower in peace?)

3. "But what I've learned is that I didn't lose her—..."

(Say how you evolved. I transformed. I softened. I became more emphatic, I carry more love, I became more powerful, not less.)

4. "One moment I'm proud of—where I showed up even though it was hard—is..."

(Was it showing up through NICU visits? Through exhaustion? Through the guilt? Through breastfeeding, when your body said no? Name it. Honor it.)

5. "I mother from a place of..."

(Fill in the blank with truth. Love. Sacred devotion. Generational healing. Whatever it is—own it.)

Optional:

Write this in your book:

"This chapter reminded me that I don't have to glow to grow. Motherhood didn't make me weaker—it revealed just how strong I already am."

Need support?

Scan the QR code to hear me guide you through this Reflect Ritual.

Because—you are the story.

And every time you show up for your babies, you rewrite the world.

You become what you believe.

— Oprah Winfrey

Chapter Seventeen

THE VISION BOARD THAT BECAME MY LIFE

IN THE BEGINNING WAS THE WORD

If you had told me in my twenties that this would be my life, I'm not sure I would've believed you. Married to the love of my life.

With two beautiful children—Mia and Samson, my Mimi and Samy.

Visiting my family in Germany, where every street corner holds a memory.

It's strange and sweet, coming full circle.

It's one of those quiet, beautiful moments, sitting with John, going through my childhood memories. I'm pulling out old pictures, letters, and little treasures from my past, laughing, remembering, telling him stories about the little girl I once was.

And then—I found it.

A small, pink suitcase.

I know this suitcase.

My childhood suitcase.

And inside? A folder.

I open it, and there, in my eleven-year-old handwriting, there's a title:

"My Dream House."

Dated September 15, 1995.

And as I flip through the pages, I feel my heart start racing. And my emotions are going wild.

Because what I see is my actual life.

I start reading, showing John, laughing at how cute and ambitious little Sisi was.

But then, the laughter stops.

Because, detail by detail, it's my life.

I wrote that I would have two kids, a girl and a boy. (Hello, Samy & Mimi!)

I wrote that my husband's name would start with a J. (Hello, John!)

I wrote that my daughter's name would start with an M. (Hello, Mimi!)

I sketched a two-story house, exactly like the one we live in.

I drew a bathtub in the exact spot and the same shape as the one we have now.

I even colored in a couch, the exact color of the couch we have today.

I am speechless.

The biggest mind-blowing part?

At eleven years old, I somehow knew that my life would look like this. How? How?

John and I just sit there, flipping through the pages in total shock.

And suddenly, it hits me.

I've always believed in God. My faith is deep and unshakable.

And when I think about it, all major religions start with the same idea: In the beginning, there was God and his creation. And I love the phrase, "In the beginning was the Word."

The word.

Because words have power.

Thoughts are one thing, but when you write them down, when you speak them out loud, when you put them into the universe, they gain momentum.

At eleven years old, I did exactly that.

I put my dream on paper. I didn't overthink it. I just wrote it down. I had never heard anything about vision boards back then.

And somehow, someway, twenty-five years later, it all came true.

If you remember, I was a little girl obsessed with America, cheerleading, football players, and the American dream.

And guess what?

I moved to America.

I married a football player. (Okay, former football player, but still. Close enough!)

I live in a beautiful house, raising my kids, building the dream I always saw in my head.

Life came full circle.

And maybe, just maybe, that's not a coincidence.

Speak it, write it, do it.

Here's the thing...

I grew up in a culture where you better keep everything to yourself, your plans, your dreams, your successes, because if you tell people, they might put the evil eye on it. They might secretly not want you to succeed. And then? Poof. It all falls apart.

I also know a lot of people still believe that. Keeping things private, staying low-key. And listen, I'm all for keeping my family life private and personal. Basically, what you see is what I allow you to see. But let me tell you, when it comes to my dreams?

I speak them out loud.

Like soooo loud.

I tell everyone.

I tell my family.

I tell my friends.

I tell my neighbors.

I tell the birds.

I tell strangers.

Damn, I even tell my enemies, lol.

I think you get my point.

A few years ago, I changed my mindset, and ever since? I've been living in momentum. Everything I truly want, I put it out there, and somehow, with determination, believing in myself and hard work, it happens.

My mother always says, "God says do the work and I will bless you."

So here's my secret: Get the word out. And the hard work. And see opportunities in everything.

Don't be afraid of the evil.

Because if God is with you, who the eff... can be against you?

If you have a dream, say it.

If you want something badly, write it down.

If you know in your soul you are meant for something bigger, tell the world.

Because words carry energy.

When you speak your dreams out loud—when you write them down, share them with others—you're not just dreaming. You're creating accountability. You're making a promise to yourself.

And in my case? Oh, I have to follow through. It's the Mediterranean-Arab in me—aka, the stubborn streak runs deep. Once I say I'm going to do something, I have to do it. It's exhausting sometimes... but it works.

You're putting it out there. Into the universe. Into God's hands. Into the path that was always meant for you.

Yes, you still have to do the work. You have to show up.

But trust me—God, the universe, divine energy, whatever name you give it—it will meet you along the way. Every time.

Because what is meant for you will always find a way to you.

Even if it takes twenty-five years to recognize.

Even if it doesn't happen the way you expected.

But one day, you might just be sitting in your childhood home, flipping through an old pink suitcase, realizing that your eleven-year-old self was right all along.

THE LESSON & REFLECT RITUAL — "In the Beginning Was the Word – The Vision Board That Became My Life"

The Lesson

Dream big. Say it, write it, believe it—because what you put out into the world will come back to you.

I always say, "Fake it till you make it." But not in the way most people think. I don't mean pretending to be something you're not—I mean acting like the person you want to become.

Want to be outgoing? Act outgoing.

Want to be successful? Move like you already are.

Want to be more giving? Start giving now.

Belief alone isn't enough—your actions have to match it.

Because if you truly believe in something, you live it. And when you start living it, you become it.

That's the secret. That's the power.

So stop waiting. Start being.

The life you want is already within you—you just have to step into it. The power of the word!

Let's reflect.

You've earned this moment.

REFLECT RITUAL – CHAPTER 17: In the Beginning Was the Word

"The Power of Speaking It Into Existence"

Your Tools:

• A quiet space

• A mirror

• Your phone (open voice memo or camera)

• 3 minutes of courage

Your Reflect Ritual (Say these out loud):

    1. "One dream I had as a child that still lives in me today is…"

(Was it a career? A place you wanted to live? A way you wanted to feel? Let her speak.)

2. "Something I once wrote down, said out loud, or prayed for—and actually saw happen—is…"

(Name it. Honor it. Remind yourself that your words are powerful.)

3. "One dream I haven't spoken out loud yet—but I'm ready to—is…"

(Declare it. Don't hold back. Let it breathe and take shape.)

4. "If I were already living the life I want, one thing I'd start doing today is…"

(Move like her. Show up like her. Dress like her. Choose like her. Start now.)

5. "The version of me who follows through on her vision boards, her prayers, her wild ideas—she is..."

(Finish this with power. She is determined. She is faithful. She is rising. Say it like you mean it.)

Optional:

Write this in your book :

"This chapter reminded me that my words carry weight. That I don't have to wait for the perfect time to believe in myself. That what I speak—I shape. And the life I want is already on its way to me."

Need support?

Scan the QR code to hear me guide you through this Reflect Ritual.

Because you are the author of your
story.

And every time you write, speak, or act on a dream—you call it
into your life.

As you start to walk on the way, the way appears.

— Rumi

CHAPTER EIGHTEEN

I WORE THE PAIN UNTIL IT BECAME MY POWER

Most days, my life was a beautiful blur of tiny footsteps, messy kitchens, sticky kisses, and bedtime stories. The rhythm of motherhood had taken over—in the best and loudest way possible. And let me be clear: not just loud. I'm talking sleepless nights, food and milk spills in my bra, and someone always yelling *"Moooom!"* like I'm Beyoncé on tour.

Motherhood was magical. Chaotic. Sacred. And sometimes? Deeply lonely.

But even in the swirl of it all, something inside me kept whispering:

You are meant for more.

Not instead of being a mother. Not instead of this life I loved so deeply. Never instead. But alongside. Because I had poured every inch of my soul into my family. My love. My body. My energy. My dreams. All of it. And yet, that old version of me—the one who dreamt big, chased bold ideas, and felt lit up by a sense of purpose beyond diapers and dinner prep—she was still alive in there. Barely, but kicking.

And I couldn't let her die.

I had fought too hard, survived too much, sacrificed so many parts of myself just to become invisible now.

I didn't want my daughter to grow up believing she had to choose between being present and being powerful. I didn't want my son to grow up thinking ambition was reserved for the workplace while love stayed at home. I wanted them to see what was possible through me. That you could build a beautiful life in more than one way.

I had always carried two worlds inside me—the warmth and soul of the Mediterranean, and the drive and clarity of the Western world. And I dreamed of blending them. Of becoming a mother who was deeply present and rooted, but also chasing big dreams with purpose and fire. I wanted it all—the slow mornings with cuddles and the thrill of chasing big dreams in leggings and lipstick.

And then, life handed me a nudge.

Every time I flew back from Europe to St. Louis, I brought outfits that made people stop mid-sentence. The compliments were constant:

"Where is that from?"

"You always look so chic—so European!"

"I wish we had pieces like this here!"

And I would smile and reply, "Germany. Vienna. Italy. You can't get it here."

At first, it was just fun. A flattered smile, a shared link to a boutique overseas. But after a while, something inside me shifted. Why not bring Europe to them?

The idea started out as a whisper and slowly took shape in my heart. I could start something here. Curate beautiful, European-inspired fashion. Build a bridge between the cultures I carried inside me. Show women that fashion could be elegant, effortless, soulful—and accessible.

And just like that, the seed was planted.

I was about to launch ShopSIHAM—an online boutique curating European-inspired pieces for women in America. Easy, right? Nope!

Starting a business in a new country with no network, no clue about U.S. business laws, and English still doing the cha-cha in my brain? Pure chaos. Google became my bestie. Trial and error became my morning routine. And thank God I had my husband, and my genius sister, Basma, by my side.

I poured everything into it—my story, my time, my sleepless nights. I dragged my sister to Vegas for three days of intense power walking and intense buying. I panicked. I overbought. I was knee-deep in summer dresses, shoes, and basic tees, thinking I had to serve everyone. Beginner's mistake: that's not how niches work.

I built my website with the help of a friend I'm still grateful for to this day. We spent weeks perfecting fonts and spacing, and obsessing over the logo and fonts. I stayed up late, Googling marketing hacks, DMing strangers, finding lawyers, and praying to all the digital gods.

And when I finally hit "publish," I was terrified—but also lit up with hope.

To celebrate the launch, I hosted a grand opening party in person. It was my first real step into the world with this dream. And to my surprise, a good number of people showed up. We had music, food, laughter, racks of clothing, and the energy was high. I sold more than I expected that day—it felt like a warm welcome into something bigger than myself.

That night I went to bed thinking, This is it. The website will blow up. It's finally happening.

But after the confetti settled, reality hit.

Nothing. No orders. No notifications. Just silence.

I kept refreshing the website like it owed me an answer. But nothing changed.

And I broke.

I questioned everything—my taste, my talent, my timing. Was I foolish? Was I delusional?

And let's be real: there's a special kind of heartbreak when the people who said they'd support you... Don't. I posted every day. Reels. Stories. Lookbooks. Vibes. I was doing the most. And still? Crickets.

That was the moment I realized—If people weren't coming to me online, I'd go to them. People needed more than a link. They needed me. My presence. My story. My hands. My voice.

Because the only time I had made money was when I had stood in front of people. When they could touch the fabric, hear my accent, ask questions, and feel the passion behind the pieces. I wasn't just selling clothes. I was selling connection. So I changed my approach. And one of the biggest things that helped me shift? Networking.

I began showing up to every opportunity I could find—markets, pop-ups, networking parties, conferences, community events. I was out there. If there was a room full of women chasing dreams, I wanted to be in it.

Networking saved my business. Period. And I want to make it loud and clear for anyone starting out: you cannot grow something alone. You need people. You need mentors. You need spaces that remind you who you are and why you started when you feel like quitting.

Two groups in particular changed the game for me.

First, Babes in Business St. Louis—a national franchise where women gather to support, uplift, and grow together. If you're reading this and you have one in your city, go. Join. These women are a beautiful community full of drive and light. They gave me a place to speak, share, and build confidence in what I was offering. I found clients, friends, and women who believed in collaboration over competition.

But the group that truly rooted me and poured so much belief into me was The Women of the Little Black Book. I cannot recommend this group enough—especially if you're in or around St. Louis. These women? They are extraordinary. It's not just about business; it's about legacy. They support each other in ways I never thought possible—no jealousy, no comparison, just heart. Real, genuine heart. Several of them became my closest friends, and I'm still moved by their kindness and strength. If you are building something and want to be surrounded by women who truly care, who truly show up, join this group. It's more than networking—it's sisterhood.

And I didn't just go to these two groups. I said yes to everything.

In that first year—really, the first year and a half—I was everywhere. I was a vendor at any event I could find. Whether it made money or not. Whether it made sense or not. I just kept showing up. Long nights. Early mornings. Little sleep. I was there. I sacrificed a lot in that season. Some events weren't really worth it. Others taught me hard lessons. But that's part of it. You learn where to go and where not to go. You find your path by walking it.

I also got involved with the International Mentoring Program, and that's actually how I started—by becoming a mentor right away for one girl who quickly became a friend. I believe in showing up. I believe in being there. I believe in helping others rise as we rise. And I will say this, for anyone building something from the ground up: have an open heart and an open mind. Be willing. Be humble. Say yes. Even if it means packing your car in the dark. Even if it means smiling through exhaustion. Even if it means walking into rooms where no one knows your name—yet.

I could never have done this alone. I had an amazing husband who helped me make it happen—who either went with me or stayed with our kids at home, or both, so I could go chase this dream. I had my family. I had my people. And I had drive.

Some nights, I came home at midnight from an event, peeled off my shoes, and tucked myself back into mom-mode before the sun even rose. And I won't lie—it was hard. It was exhausting. But it was worth it.

If I could give one piece of advice? Show up.

Show up to everything. Be a vendor. Put your name out there. Put your product out there. Most importantly: put yourself out there.

Ask for opportunities. Don't wait. Don't hope someone notices you.

Want to be on TV? Email the producer.

Want to be in a magazine? DM the editor.

Want to collaborate? Ask the business owner.

Want to speak on stage? Pitch yourself.

Whatever it is—ask. Ask with heart. Ask with confidence. Ask even if your hands are shaking. Because closed mouths don't get fed.

Another big turning point for me was stepping into public speaking. I started saying yes to panels, community events, podcasts—any space where I could share my story. And the more I shared, the more I connected. The more I connected, the more my brand grew. Not just in reach, but in impact. Speaking became one of the most powerful tools I had—not just to promote ShopSI-HAM, but to inspire. To remind other women they could rise too. It helped me heal parts of myself while giving others permission to stand tall in their own story. And it anchored me even more deeply in my purpose.

Your story matters.

Your face matters.

You matter.

Be your brand. Live it. Breathe it. Wear it. If your brand doesn't feel like you, it's not aligned. But if it does—if it's truly you—then don't hold back. People don't buy from businesses. They buy from people. They want a piece of your heart. So give it to them.

And always—always—help others along the way.

Don't rise alone. Rise with others. Cheer them on. Lift them up. That's where the real success lives.

Collaboration over competition. Always.

I stood hour after hour with a smile, pitching my story, selling my pieces, learning how to make real connections—not just clicks. I went on Instagram stories even though I felt SO awkward at first.

My accent, my voice, my nerves—ugh. But I showed up anyway. Every day.

Post by post. Reel by reel. Moment by moment.

I fought to be seen.

And slowly... it started working.

One customer became two.

Two became ten.

It didn't happen overnight. But it happened through sweat, soul, and showing up.

Still, something inside me whispered, This isn't enough. Not for you. Not yet. Because I wasn't raised to just take. I was raised to give.

My parents taught me that giving back was not a thing you do—it's a way you live. A duty. A blessing. And whatever I was building had to mean more than just fabric and style. It had to carry purpose.

I knew I wanted to give back. That was always part of the dream. I had thought about kids—kids with cancer, kids with special needs. So many beautiful causes. I kept telling myself I needed to decide soon which organization I would partner with, because giving back felt urgent.

Then one night, I was half-asleep, in that space between rest and thought, and it hit me. Like someone—or something—whispered into my soul.

Burn survivors. What about children with scars?

I shot up in bed. My heart raced.

It was like a higher power reached in and turned on the light.

How had I never thought of this before?

I mean—I had scars. I was burned. I lived my entire life covering them up, ignoring them, faking confidence I didn't always feel. But what about the kids who couldn't pretend yet? What about the children who felt like they had to hide?

Were they being seen?

Did they have support?

Were they told they were beautiful?

The next morning, I started researching. I didn't know what I would find, but I knew I had to do something. And that same day, I discovered a nonprofit in St. Louis that supports burn survivors. I picked up the phone.

And from that moment on, ShopSIHAM became something more.

It became a mission. A purpose. A light.

A portion of every sale would go toward supporting that nonprofit.

And for the first time ever, I began to tell my full story. My scars. My survival. My why.

And then, I met Kanisha—a burn survivor, just like me. The first one I had ever met in my entire life.

I don't think people truly understand what that means. I grew up in Germany feeling like an alien in my own skin. Everywhere I went, I carried my scars like a secret I never got to share. I never had someone who understood what it felt like to walk into a room and feel the stares. Or to sit in a locker room, trying to change quickly, hoping no one would ask questions. I never had someone who just got it. And then—there she was. A radiant soul who worked with the burn organization, I had recently connected my shop to. From the moment we spoke, it was like something inside of me shifted. Like finding a missing piece to a puzzle I didn't even know I was still trying to solve.

Meeting her caught me completely off guard. I thought I was just supporting a good cause—partnering my shop with a nonprofit, attending some group meetings, maybe visiting a retreat. I was doing it naively, just wanting to help, to show up. But somewhere in the middle of those conversations, hugs, and shared experiences, a door opened that I never meant to open. And when it did... everything poured out. Decades of buried emotion, of being "strong" and "fine," cracked open like a dam.

I went through something that felt like deep, unexpected therapy. I cried. A lot. I reflected more than I ever had. I started thinking about my scars—not just how they looked, but how they lived inside me. And the truth that hit me hardest? I hated them. I hated my scars more than I had ever admitted out loud. I spent years dreaming of ways to cover them, erase them, pretend they weren't there.

Especially in my childhood and teenage years, the shame ran so deep I couldn't even name it. I remember the dread I felt every time I was around people, especially if there was a cute boy nearby. I'd silently pray, Please, please don't let anyone mention my scars. Please don't let them ask. Don't embarrass me. It was a quiet fear I carried everywhere. I always hoped I could slip by unnoticed, invisible in that one way. And yet, there were always moments, like at swimming pools, surrounded by classmates, carefree and laughing. I still went. I still wore my swimsuit. I still joined the fun. But deep down, I was bracing myself.

Kids would stare. They'd point. They'd ask loud, unfiltered questions like, "Mom, what's on her leg?" or "What happened to her stomach?" That fear never left me. And the worst part? The boy I had a crush on—the same one I mentioned in an earlier chapter—he was often there too. He grew up with me. He knew I had scars. But even then, the shame of someone saying it out loud, of making me a spectacle in front of him, felt unbearable. I would laugh it off or ignore it, but it always stung.

The shame didn't stop with the kids. I heard things from adults, too, people referring to me as the burned one: "Oh... is this your burned daughter?"

It cut me deeply every single time. My mother, fierce and protective, would instantly snap. She'd shut it down like a lioness guarding her cub. I adored her for that. And yet, I'd always try to calm her down, brushing it off with a smile—"Don't worry, Mama. I don't care."

But now, writing this, I wonder if I really didn't care... or if I had just gotten good at pretending.

People always say, "Live outside your comfort zone." But I feel like I've lived my whole life outside the comfort zone. I was never given one. Because of my scars. Because of my background. Because of my skin. I've always been the different one. Always had to adapt, survive, smile through things that didn't feel okay.

So, yes, now, as an adult, I crave that comfort zone sometimes. I crave a space to just be. But ironically, it's also where I've found my power. Outside the lines. At the edge of pain. In the fire.

I remember being a teenager, thinking maybe I'd get a tattoo to hide the scars. Anything to feel more like everyone else. And years later, while backpacking in Thailand, I found myself at a full moon party.

Everyone painted their bodies in wild colors. So I painted my scars. Covered my leg in neon swirls and patterns. For one night, I felt invisible in the best way. No one stared. They just thought I was having fun like everyone else. I wore shorts and didn't twist my leg or hide. I just... existed. And it felt like freedom. For a split second, I believed, maybe I could live like this forever. But that moment, that temporary relief, was born from the deepest place of shame. And that shame had shaped more of my life than I was willing to admit.

And I'll never forget what happened when I was about eighteen or nineteen. I had a boyfriend—someone I really liked. Someone I thought liked me, too. And then one day, he saw my scars... and disappeared. Ghosted me completely. I brushed it off—teenage boys, right? But a few weeks later, I learned the truth from a friend: he had dumped me because of my scars. It hit me like a punch to the stomach. Of course, I laughed it off. I acted like I didn't care. Like he wasn't worth my time. But deep down? It broke me. And it happened again. And again. That silent wondering, Am I lovable like this?

For the first time, through this community—and Kanisha—I realized how much of that pain I had never dealt with. I had survived, yes. I had even thrived. But I had also tucked away layer upon layer of heartbreak, rejection, and self-doubt. And now, those layers were unraveling.

For the first time, I began to understand that just because I had functioned through life—confident, stylish, bold on the outside—didn't mean I had truly healed. Yes, I always wore the fashion I loved. I didn't let my scars stop me. But if I'm honest, I used to twist my legs when I sat, subtly angling them away so people couldn't really see. Even in my boldness, there was always a flicker of hiding. I didn't know it then, but I carried shame quietly, like a whisper behind the clothes.

Kanisha helped change that. Being around her made me want to stand taller. To show my scars—not just accept them, but own them. When we did model shoots, I didn't try to pose around them. I showed them. I led with them. And I wasn't just fine, I was proud. They became a part of my power, not my pain. I started to wear them like a crown.

Because here's the truth: I turned what once felt like the biggest challenge of my life into my absolute superpower. And while I'm writing this chapter, something inside me is shifting again. This book, in so many ways, feels like therapy. I'm realizing things I never let myself say out loud. Like, how grateful I am for the way my mother raised us. She was tough—no pity party, no excuses. She wouldn't let us wallow in sadness. At times, I thought: This is a little too Mediterranean, a little too intense. But now? I get it. She was preparing us for a world that can be cruel. A world that doesn't always show grace. She raised warriors. And Mama, if you're reading this—I love you. So much. Thank you for making me strong enough to stand in rooms that once terrified me. And thank you for still being the lioness who would burn the world down to protect me.

To my parents, my siblings—I love you endlessly.

To my husband, the man who sees me, who loves me exactly as I am, who looks at my scars like they're nothing more than skin—thank you. You've been a mirror of unconditional love, and you helped me heal in ways you don't even know.

All of you—my family, Kanisha, my community—helped me put the broken pieces back together. And now? Even if there were a chance to erase them, I wouldn't. My scars tell my story. They are mine. They are me. They are the ink on the pages of my life—the parts I once wanted to cross out are now the lines I read with pride.

And wow... now I'm sitting here crying.

Okay—deep breath. Enough about me.

Let's go back to the story. Because just when I thought I had poured all of myself into healing, something new began to bloom.

As ShopSIHAM grew, something inside me stirred again. A deeper longing to create something even more personal. Something that didn't just represent the women I serve, but the people who fuel my every breath. My family. My home. My fire.

That's how MISAJO was born.

Mi for Mimi.
Sa for Samy.
Jo for John.

MISAJO became my own clothing line, designed, curated, and produced with love. A true blend of heart and style. I even launched MISAJO Sports, my activewear line designed for all women, immigrant women, moms, women with scars, women of every size and background.

MISAJO became my love letter to strength and resilience.

What began as a personal journey of healing, of reclaiming my confidence, of learning to love the parts of me I once hid—slowly grew into something much bigger. Something sacred.

And then something unexpected happened: women started asking me for more. They didn't just want the clothes—they wanted the confidence behind the clothes. They wanted to know how I carried myself, how I styled my life after pain, how I stayed strong. They wanted coaching, style advice, fitness, and nutrition guidance. They wanted transformation.

The media started to notice, too. Podcasts reached out. Magazines published my story. I even made it on the cover, yes, I'm a cover girl. All the local TV stations wanted to feature me. Honestly, it felt surreal. I had so many interviews and appearances. It is truly amazing. Because what started with clothes became a calling.

That's when ShopSIHAM evolved. It became more than a brand. It became a movement.

A place where women from all walks of life could come together, be seen, be celebrated, and feel powerful.

Especially women with scars—visible or invisible. Because let's be real, scarred women are still wildly underrepresented in fashion. But not in my world. Never in my world.

It started with a simple idea: a brand photoshoot in my basement.

I invited women of all ages, all sizes, all backgrounds, all stories, visible scars and invisible ones.

Many walked in shy, unsure of themselves.

But they left radiant. Empowered. Connected.

They shared their truths.

They lifted each other up.

They built something beautiful together.

That day, a community was born.

We called it *Sisterhood*—a safe space where women could support one another, rise together, and feel like they truly belonged.

You can still join us there today. The movement lives on through a Facebook group that we just started, The Confidence Collective.

And you know what's funny? This all started from nothing. Just an idea. A feeling. A basement. A girl with a dream and a story to tell.

I came from that girl with no degree at all. I worked my way up, earned every credential, every single degree, traveled the world, lived in different cultures, and eventually made my way here—America—where I built something from the ground up. And now, it's come full circle.

Fashion was my first language.

It made me feel beautiful when I didn't believe I was.

It gave me confidence when nothing else could.

As a little girl, it was the only place I felt in control.

As a burn survivor, it helped me reclaim my reflection.

And now? Fashion is how I help other women rise.

What began as my love for fabrics, color, and style turned into a mission: to empower women, especially those who carry deep scars, whether you can see them or not.

What started as childhood dress-up became a calling:

To walk beside women as they step into their power.

To help them feel strong, beautiful, and whole.

To show them that their past does not define them, but it can refine them.

It became about so much more than clothes.

It became about helping women see themselves again, not through society's eyes, but through their own.

To own their story. To rewrite their worth. To embody their strength.

I've loved butterflies since I was a little girl.

One day, I heard something that stayed with me:

"Not every caterpillar becomes a butterfly. Some never realize they can."

But those who believe? They break free.

That's how I see you.

You have it in you.

You just have to believe in your transformation.

That's my mission.

To help women become butterflies in a world full of caterpillars.

What started with a few European pieces became:

MISAJO – a full fashion line

MISAJO Sports – activewear made for women who rise

Transformation Coaching – style, health, and confidence

A Growing Network – workshops, events, and an ambassador program

A Community of Warriors – diverse, powerful, unstoppable women

And this?

This is only the beginning.

Because if there's one thing I've learned, it's this:

You can rise from the ashes.

You can heal.

You can grow.

And you can turn your scars into your superpower.

That, my friend, is the real flex.

THE LESSON & REFLECT RITUAL

The Lesson:

Your scars do not disqualify you—they qualify you.

They don't make you less worthy. They make you real.

You can hold grief and grit.

You can be healing and still be powerful.

You can cry and lead.

You can wear your past and still walk into your future like a queen.

You don't have to be healed to begin.

You don't have to be fearless to rise.

And you sure as hell don't need to be flawless to be powerful.

You have been taught to hide the parts of you that make people uncomfortable.

Your scars, your pain, your softness, your rage.

But those parts? That's where the gold is. That's where your story lives.

The things you once begged to erase may become your greatest gifts.

The scars you hated might become the very source of your strength.

The moments that made you feel broken are the same ones that make you brave.

You thought you were too damaged, too different, too much?

No, my love. You are just too powerful to fit into boxes that were never built for you.

Real confidence isn't about pretending nothing ever hurt you.

It's about standing tall because of what hurt you, and rising anyway.

Let's reflect.

You've earned this moment.

REFLECT RITUAL – CHAPTER 18: I Wore The Pain Until It Became My Power

"My Scars, My Strength, My Story"

Your Tools:

• A quiet space

• A mirror

• Your phone (open voice memo or camera)

• 3 minutes of courage

Your Reflect Ritual (Say these out loud):

> 1. "One part of my story or my body I used to hide or be
>   ashamed of was..."

(a scar, a story, or a moment that shaped you. Let it surface.)

2. "I used to believe this part of me meant I was..."

(Too broken? Not enough? Unlovable? Say the old story. Then let
it go.)

3."But what I now know is that this part of me actually makes
me..."

(Powerful. Compassionate. Brave. Unique. Whatever truth you
now see—own it.)

4."A moment where I stood tall in my truth—even when it was
hard—was..."

(Was it starting something? Telling your story? Choosing visibility over silence?)

5. "I no longer twist, shrink, or hide because today I know that I am..."

(Finish with power. I am whole. I am radiant. I am beautifully unedited.)

Optional:

Write this in your book:

"This chapter reminded me that healing doesn't mean hiding. It means honoring every piece of who I am. My scars are not what I need to erase—they're what I needed to embrace."

Need support?

Scan the QR code to hear me guide you through this Reflect Ritual.

Because you are not your pain.

You are what rose from it.

And every time you stand in your story, you light the way for someone else to rise, too.

In order to be irreplaceable, one must always be different.

— Coco Chanel

Chapter Nineteen

STEPPING ONSTAGE FOR LITTLE SISI:

FOR EVERY WOMAN WITH SCARS

So here I am.

A mother of two. A devoted wife. An entrepreneur. A business owner. A Stylist. A transformation coach.

A woman who empowers other women.

I'm living my best life in America, running a business that reflects who I am, lifting women up, proving that you can be fully present for your family while chasing your dreams. And as if that weren't enough, I have my own styling segment, Styling with Sisi, on KMOV, Channel 4, every second Friday of the month. An opportunity I was honored to be asked to do. That's how much of a name I've built for myself in St. Louis.

And every time I step into that studio, every time I share style and transformation tips, I feel an overwhelming sense of pride. Because my segment isn't just about clothes. It's about styling your life, your confidence, your mindset, your health, your presence.

But if you know me, you know I'm never satisfied with just one dream.

As I approached forty, I found myself asking: What's next?

For years, I had been fascinated by bodybuilding. Ever since I met my husband, a competitor with the physique of a literal Greek god (but let's not get lost in that again), I had admired the discipline, dedication, and transformation the sport required.

And deep down, I always wondered... Could I do it, too?

For the longest time, it was never the right moment. Until now.

I wanted to drop those last pregnancy pounds—not because I had to, but because I wanted to. I wanted to look great and feel great. I wanted to prove to myself that I could do something extraordinary. But most of all?

I wanted to step on that stage for Little Sisi.

The little girl who grew up feeling invisible.

The little girl who thought she wasn't good enough.

The little girl who hid her scars, doubted herself, and let the voices in her head tell her she would never be enough.

This wasn't just about a competition. It was about proving to every woman with scars—visible or invisible—that we are powerful.

The biggest, most emotional part of stepping on that stage wasn't about winning. It was about owning my scars.

Not hiding them. Not covering them. Owning them.

Because I wanted to be a symbol for all burn survivors.

I wanted every woman with scars—inside or out—to look at me and think, If she can do it, I can too.

I wanted my kids to be proud of me.

That was my ultimate goal.

Because in the world of sports—especially bodybuilding—backgrounds don't matter. The gym doesn't care where you're from. The weights don't discriminate. The stage welcomes anyone who dares to show up.

And I was ready to show up.

I knew I needed guidance.

Even though my husband is a coach, I wanted a female mentor—someone who knew the bikini competition world inside and out. So I found a pro competitor, hired her, and started my prep.

And let me tell you, this was no joke.

Twelve weeks of strict nutrition. Brutal workouts. Discipline like I had never known.

But it wasn't just my body that transformed.

My mind did, too.

This journey was more than just training for a bodybuilding competition.

It was therapy for my soul.

Memories surfaced—emotions I had buried for years came rushing back.

Some mornings, mid-cardio, I had to stop and just cry.

But it wasn't sadness.

It was release.

It was healing.

It was pride.

Because I could finally tell Little Sisi, Look at us. Look what we are capable of. Look—we can do hard things.

And the power of discipline? Unreal.

I always tell people, eff motivation. Motivation is bullshit.

Motivation is temporary.

Discipline is what gets you up when motivation is gone. Discipline is what builds a champion. Discipline is what keeps you moving forward, no matter what.

And the craziest part? Once you embrace discipline, you start loving it.

As a mom, as an entrepreneur, having structure and a driving force makes life easier.

I could stand back and say: I am so damn proud of myself. Not in an arrogant way. In a way that says, I earned this.

Because I did this.

Me.

Little Sisi, the girl who once felt invisible, did something extraordinary.

I trained for months.

I built a strong, powerful body.

I stepped onto a stage, half-naked, showing my scars, owning my story.

And I did it coming from a culture where this isn't even acceptable for women.

That? That's a victory bigger than any trophy.

Finally, the day had arrived.

The big day that I told you about at the beginning of this book.

We checked into the hotel. Got spray-tanned (which, surprise, made me nauseous—turns out I'm allergic, but I powered through). My amazing husband, my ride-or-die, was right there by my side.

Pre-judging flew by in the morning, and then the evening show came.

And before I knew it, I was back under those bright lights.

My leg was shaking. My arms were trembling. My smile was so wide I swore my face would need medical attention.

I stood there, judges watching, a sea of people staring.

And then I heard it.

"Third place."

Not hiding. Not covering up.

Winning.

I clutched that medal, and for a split second, my whole life flashed before me.

The struggles. The doubts. The scars.

The sleepless nights. The fear.

The years I thought I wasn't enough.

And yet...

Here I was.

One of the proudest me moments of my life.

And it's only the beginning.

I will continue to spread empowerment, love, and light.

To help others see their power.

Because we all deserve to rise.

Please, never let anyone dim your light or make you believe you're not capable.

Start your transformation journey.

We are all caterpillars.

And the choice is ours: stay where we are or become the butterfly we were always meant to be.

Spread your wings.

Step into your power.

And take the world for yourself.

Xoxo,
Sisi

For the Powerhouse Who Just Finished This Last Chapter (Yes, YOU)

THE LESSON & REFLECT RITUAL

The Lesson

Your scars are not your weakness—they're your superpower.

You don't need perfect timing, the perfect body, or a flawless past.

You need fire. You need faith. You need reps.

You need to show up.

That's the secret no one tells you:

Discipline builds power. Confidence comes from courage. And courage? You create it through action.

What you practice, you become.

So practice being unstoppable. Practice being seen. Practice being your full damn self.

If a mama of two, a two-time immigrant, a stranger in a new country, and a burn survivor (yup, still me) can walk on stage in a sparkly bikini—with scars out and a grin so big it could power a city—then sister, what are you waiting for?

No is not an option. Shrinking is not an option.

The world doesn't need less of you. It needs all of you.

You weren't born to hide. You were born to own your stage.

And yes, this is about more than stepping into a bikini.

It's about stepping into your power.

And you don't need permission.

You just need a little hype, a lot of heart, and the decision to begin.

Let's reflect.

You've earned this moment.

REFLECT RITUAL – CHAPTER 19: Own Your Stage

"Your Power Is Already In You—Now Go Use It."

Your Tools:

• A quiet space

• A mirror

• Your phone (open voice memo or camera)

• 3 minutes of courage

Your Reflect Ritual (Say these out loud):

1. "One moment in my life where I was brave, bold, or just a total badass was…"

(Yes, starting over counts. So does choosing peace. So does putting on lipstick when you wanted to hide.)

2. "A time I showed up—even when I was scared, tired, or unsure—was…"

(You did it anyway. Say it out loud. Let her hear you.)

3. "One thing I've always wanted to do—but told myself I wasn't ready for—is…"

(No more hiding. Name it. Claim it.)

4. "What I now know is... I don't have to be perfect to be powerful, because..."

(Your truth goes here. Your breakthrough. Your reminder.)

5. "I will no longer shrink to fit into spaces that weren't made for me. Because today, I know that I..."

(Finish this with power: I am worthy. I am visible. I am rising. Say it like you mean it.)

Optional:

Write this in your book:

"This chapter reminded me that I don't need to be flawless to rise.

I don't need permission to lead.

My scars, my story, my strength—they were never a setback.

They were always my wings."

Need support?

Scan the QR code to hear me guide
you through this Reflect Ritual.

Because this is your time.

You've spent enough years shrinking.

Now rise.

Fly.

And take up your space, sister.

The world and I have been waiting for you.

My parents in the 1970s—mom on the left,
dad on the right. Young, bold, and beautiful.

Me on my dad's shoulders with my brother and sister in our shared kids' bedroom, old apartment in Munich, Germany (circa 1985).

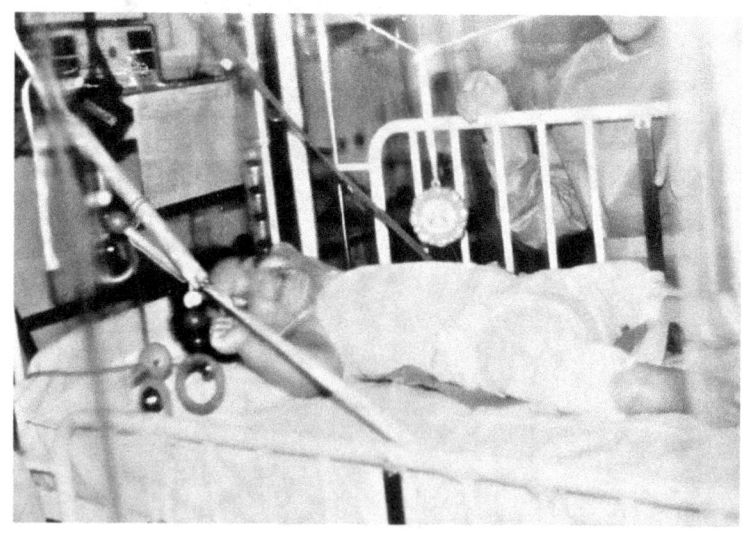

May 1985, Munich hospital ICU. Me wrapped in burn dressings, smiling in bed just after the accident.

Winter 1985, Munich. Playing in the snow with
my sister and mom, all in snowsuits.

Summer 1986, Morocco. My mom holding me
at the beach, after my burn recovery.

Morocco family gathering. I'm in the center with my sister behind me, brother next to her, surrounded by aunts and uncles.

Morocco again. I'm the smallest one on the left with Aunt Saida (center) and Aunt Raja next to her.

Me, my sister, and brother dancing in our Munich bedroom, fully in our element—pretending to be singers and having a blast.

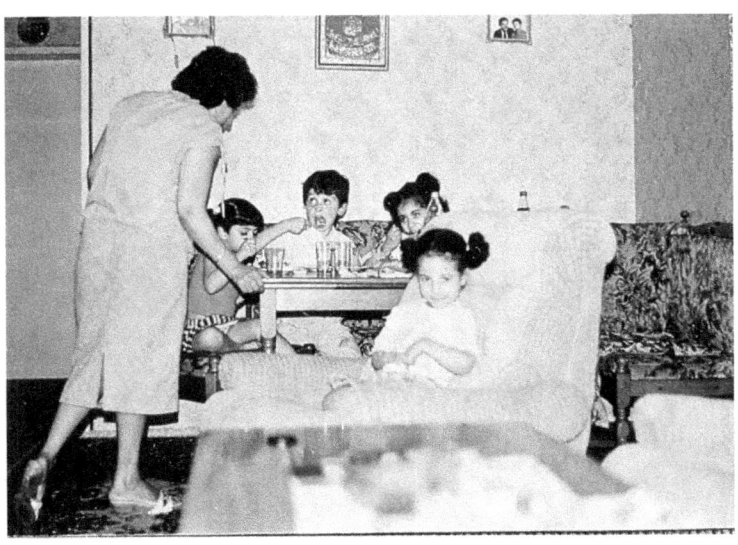

My birthday, around 1990. I'm sitting on the recliner; behind me are my mom, Mona (my best friend), my sister's friend, and my sister—in our Munich living room.

Me and my sister in pajamas on a cozy Sunday, messy afros and all—our classic living room in Munich.

My kindergarten birthday. I'm wearing a crown, and Patrick (the boy who teased me) is wiggling on the chair nearby.

Beach day in Morocco. I'm sitting on my mom's lap
in a swimsuit, happily sucking on a lollipop.

Another birthday. From left to right: Mona, me, my sister,
Basma, and her friend—small but sweet gathering.

Summer 1990, Tunisia. My first time there—
6 years old, posing at the beach in Sousse.

Probably age 10, writing in my diary in the
Munich bedroom I shared with my sister.

Day 3 in Thailand — when it all began.
From left to right: Me, John (JT), and my sister, Basma
riding together in a tuk-tuk.

Another magical day in Thailand.
From left to right: Basma, John (JT), and me — soaking in the beauty.

The morning after our very first date.
Sitting at the beach in Thailand, barely knowing each other
—but something already felt so familiar.

Our trip to Vietnam.

Our last few hours in Thailand, after just a few days
together, but it felt like we'd known each other forever.

Vietnam — reunited.
A month and a half later, we found our way back to each other in
Vietnam, finally together again after all that waiting.

Henna night magic.
My mama, glowing with pride, making the most delicious food. And next to her—my childhood friend Rose, one of my forever girls.

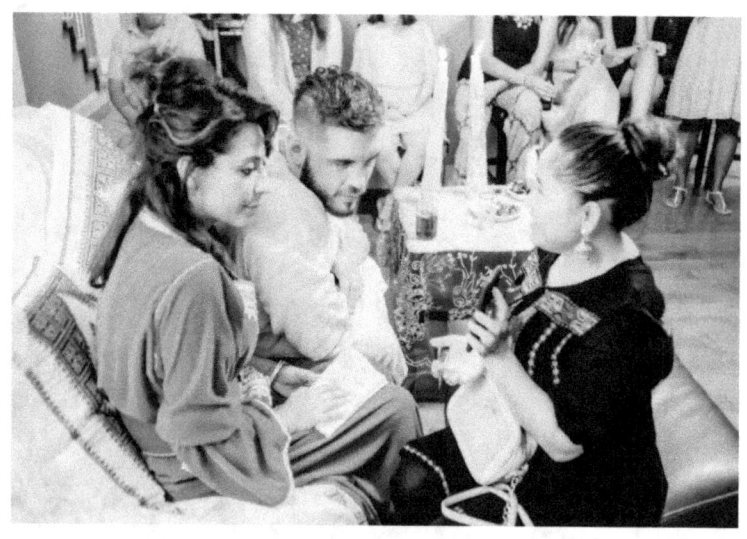

Planning our henna.
Side by side, getting the scoop on what kind of henna we want.

Me on the Amaria, in my kaftan lifted by JT's football friends—
Moroccan music, laughter, and pure joy. A queen for the night.

JT on the Amaria, rocking his Moroccan outfit, carried by his
boys. A king moment we'll never forget.

JT and I on the Amaria, dressed in our Moroccan best, laughing, dancing, and living our fairytale.

JT and I and our two kids, in
St. Louis, Missouri—our full-circle moment.

ABOUT THE AUTHOR

Sisi Surgant is a proud Moroccan-Tunisian, born and raised in Germany, and a double immigrant whose journey has been anything but ordinary. A burn survivor from a young age, she turned pain into purpose, and scars into symbols of resilience.

She earned her degrees later in life and traveled to over forty countries, collecting stories, cultures, and inspiration from around the globe. Her heart led her even further—while backpacking in Thailand, she met the love of her life, which brought her across the ocean to St. Louis, where she now lives with her husband and their two beautiful children.

Sisi is a stylist, fashion entrepreneur (founder of ShopSIHAM), transformation coach, speaker, and competitive bodybuilding athlete. She's also the creator of MISAJO Sports—an activewear line built to empower women through movement and confidence.

With every project, post, and piece of clothing, she builds bridges between cultures and reminds others that their story is their power.

Connect with Sisi:

Website: ShopSIHAM.com

Website: sisisurgant.com

Email: info@ShopSIHAM.com

Instagram: @sisi.sur

ACKNOWLEDGEMENTS

To my husband, John—

You have been my rock since day one. The calm to my fire, the laughter in my chaos, the soft place I never knew I needed until I landed there. Your love has made me stronger, bolder, and more grounded in who I truly am. But more than that—you've made me *feel* safe enough to be all of me. All the time. There's this one line in the song *Soul Sister* that always makes me cry: *"I can be myself now finally. In fact, there's nothing I can't be. I want the world to see you be with me."* And that's how I feel about you. With you, there's nothing I can't be. You see me. Truly. Through my scars, through my joy, through my doubts and dreams and quiet moments of fear—you love every part of me.

You've made me a better woman, a happier woman, a more loving woman. You've made me believe that fairytales don't have to be perfect—they just have to be real. This life, this family, this love we've built... It's my everything. I will never stop thanking God for giving me *you*.

I'm so grateful to walk this life with such a humble, faithful man by my side. What a gift. What a blessing. What a love.

To my children, Mimi and Samy—

You are the kind of love I didn't know was possible. The kind that cracks you wide open and rebuilds you stronger, softer, and braver than you've ever been. You didn't just change my life—you became it. Mimi, my fierce little storm wrapped in glitter and sunshine. Samy, my gentle soul with the healing hugs and wise eyes. You are my balance, my why, my every breath. Every dream I chase, every word I write, every risk I take—I do it with you in my heart. Thank you for choosing me to be your mama. You are my forever, my legacy, my greatest joy.

To Mama and Baba, my parents—

Thank you for raising me with unwavering love and strength. You gave me a sense of home that's unshakable—I've always known that no matter what happens in life, I can come back to you, and you'll be there. Always. You taught me how to work hard, love harder, and walk through this world with grace, grit, and resilience. You gave me an edge, a toughness, a street-smart way of thinking that has carried me through so much. You showed me the real meaning of *family first*—a bond so deep, so fiercely loyal, that it became part of who I am.

You supported me through my degree, through my wild Australia backpacking days, and through every dream I dared to speak out loud. You believed in every single crazy idea I ever had—and there's truly nothing I can ever do to repay you for that. Nothing. I carry everything you've given me with pride and gratitude every single day.

To my brother, Zouhaier—

You've been my quiet guardian angel. You gave me a sense of safety and strength that I held onto, even when you didn't know you were doing it. Thank you for always being there, in your way, with your steady presence and big heart.

Growing up, just knowing you were my big brother gave me confidence. Your presence made me feel protected in a world that didn't always feel safe. And even now, as a grown woman, that bond still gives me comfort. Knowing you're there will always be one of life's greatest gifts.

To my sister, Basma—

Because of you, I never felt like I needed many friends—you were always my best friend. The bond we share is one of the greatest gifts a girl can receive. No matter where life takes us, I know I have my person forever. You get me with just one look, and that kind of love is rare and priceless.

The love you gave me growing up felt like a second mother's—protective, fierce, and full of grace. You've seen every silly part of me, every weakness, and loved me even harder for it. You've helped me heal in places I didn't even know were wounded. You've always protected me like a lioness, shielding me from pain I didn't even know was near. And for that... I will forever be grateful.

To my nephew, Jamal—

I love you as if you were my own. Watching the boy you were and the man you're becoming fills me with pride I can hardly put into words. You have a forever place in my heart.

You're such a kind soul, a calm and steady presence—even in the midst of chaos, there's something about you that feels like a safe place. I'm endlessly proud of the young man you're becoming, and I can't wait to see what life has in store for you. And don't forget—no matter how tall you grow, I'll always see you as our little Jamusi.

To my uncle, Abdu—

Even if I didn't talk much about you in the book, you'll always have a special place in my heart. You were such a big part of my childhood—more like a brother and an uncle in one. You were nerve-wracking sometimes with your wild humor, and you definitely tested us—mentally, emotionally, but you also taught us how to be sharp, resilient, and quick on our feet. You gave us edge. And despite it all (or maybe because of it), I love you so much. Thank you for being my "many nanny," picking me up from kindergarten, teasing us, loving us, and being unforgettable in the best way.

To my aunt, Saida—

I know I never mentioned in this book that I once lived in Morocco for a whole year as a child—it just didn't feel like the right time to tell that story. But during that year, we all lived together under one roof—my grandparents, aunts, uncles, —and even though you were still young, you took care of me like I was your own. You were like a second mama to me, showing me tenderness even while navigating your own heartbreaks and growing pains. I saw your strength most of all. Thank you for loving me through it, for making me feel chosen, and for staying etched in my heart.

To my uncle, Mokhtar—

You left this world 1.5 years ago, but you'll never leave my heart. So much of what I know and feel when it comes to music—reggae, Bollywood, Tracy Chapman, that soul-stirring sound—I got from you. You were a free spirit who taught me that mindset is power, and that no illness, pain, or darkness can touch the freedom of a strong, joyful mind. I still think of you when I listen to Bob Marley or Tracy Chapman, when I choose light over fear. Thank you for your love, your wisdom, and your presence that still lingers like a song that never ends.

To my uncles, aunts, and grandparents in Morocco—

Some of you are still with us, and some have become memories and stories that live on in our hearts. But all of you helped shape the woman I am today. Thank you for the summers filled with tradition, connection, and culture—for the couscous Fridays, the chaos, the drama, the freedom, the love—and for the tough lessons, too. It wasn't always easy, but it made me street-smart, sharp, creative, and bold. You taught us to think outside the box, to survive, to adapt. Even from across oceans, I feel your impact. I always will.

To my family in Tunisia—

You impacted my childhood and young adulthood more than you'll ever know. In the most loving way, you showed me that family is a sacred bond and that no matter what, family always comes first. Your love, your loyalty, and your presence helped build the foundation of who I am. I carry you with me, always.

To my parents-in-law—

Thank you for welcoming me with open hearts and loving me as your own in a country that once felt so far from home. Your warmth, kindness, and quiet strength gave me a sense of belonging and safety when I needed it most. I will always be grateful for the love you've shown me.

To my sister-in-law and brother-in-law—

I'm so thankful to have you both in my life. Gaining siblings in this chapter of my journey has been such a gift. Knowing you're there, cheering me on and having my back, means more than words can say.

To your amazing children—my nephews and niece—

You are loved beyond measure. Watching you grow fills my heart with joy, and I hope you always feel how deeply you are cherished and loved.

To my childhood best friend, Mona—

You were my first friend, my mirror, and my safe place. You helped me in ways you probably never even knew. You opened my eyes to joy, to courage, to the idea that there was more out there for me beyond the rules and expectations I lived under. Because of you, I learned to loosen up, take chances, and believe in myself a little more. You pushed me—sometimes literally!—out of my comfort zone, and into laughter, adventure, and self-discovery. You were a bigger gift to me than you'll ever realize, and a light in my childhood I'll never forget.

To Kanisha—

You grew on me like a sister. As a fellow burn survivor, you held up a mirror I didn't know I needed. I always *thought* I was confident in my scars—until I met you. Somehow, just by being you, old layers cracked open. You stood with me while hidden trauma bubbled up, and you showed me what it looks like to live bold, visible, and whole. Because of you, I stopped "managing" my scars and started owning them. Your friendship, your presence, and your power helped me step deeper into my purpose and build a business that lifts other survivors, too. I love you, sis.

To My Friends—Near and Far

To my childhood friends in Germany—thank you for seeing something in me worth holding onto. Your love still reaches me, and I'm so grateful we're still in touch after all these years.

To the friends I met later in life, in classrooms and cafés, in moments of becoming—thank you for cheering me on across oceans and standing by me through all the chapters.

And to my St. Louis crew—your open arms, your laughter, your love… you helped turn a foreign place into a real home. I'll never forget it.

Thank you, friends. You are stitched into the fabric of my story. Always and forever, I carry you with me.

To my incredible editor and friend, Shelly—

You've always been a friend, but through this process, you became an even closer one. Thank you for treating my story with such care and heart—it means more to me than you'll ever know.

You honored my voice and took the way I wrote as a gift, not something to fix. And still, you cleaned up the chaos—polishing the grammar, chasing down commas, calming the exclamation marks, and helping this immigrant girl's words shine.

But more than that—you never let me stay on the surface. You gently, persistently poked, prodded, and questioned until the real story poured out. You pulled truth from the corners I tried to skip over, and I'm so glad you did. Because of you, this book didn't just heal—it transformed me. And for that, I'll be forever thankful.

To my friend Angel—

Thank you for seeing something in me before I fully saw it in myself. Your encouragement planted a seed that grew into these pages. I'm deeply grateful for your belief in my story, your support behind the scenes, and for giving me the space to bring this dream to life. Your impact runs deeper than you know.

To the beautiful souls who read my early drafts—

Your feedback, encouragement, and honest reflections helped me see this book more clearly. I'm so thankful for your hearts and your time. You are part of my inner circle, my trusted people—some of my closest friends—and it meant the world to share this vulnerable journey with you.

To every person who prayed for me, believed in me, or held space for this dream—

You're in these pages more than you know.

Thank you, from the bottom of my heart.